HIS Story

A couple's journey of love and loss ——

and a far greater Grace

SHAWN WARD

Printed in the United States of America by Kindle Direct Publishing

First Printing, 2018

ISBN: 9781730969225

To all the women, men,
and families
who in some way share in this story . . .

CONTENTS

Acknowledgments

As I consider the acknowledgments, there are many who have traveled on this journey, who have helped me tremendously, in different ways, to tell my story.

First of all, thank you to Scott and Sandi Tompkins, who took on the job of reviewing my first draft and offered important advice and great counsel for needed changes and direction. Thank you, Sandi, for introducing me to this "author's world," educating me on some of my very "firsts," and connecting me with some of the important people who would help me further on my journey to write, and to finish, this book. I love and appreciate you both.

Thank you, Kay ben-Avraham—you graciously took the editing mantle from near the start to the very finish, offering not only your talents as an incredibly competent editor but also offering, from your heart, wise counsel and direction that allowed the finished book to become what is. You have prayed with me, cried with me, laughed with me on this journey, and your contributions have been invaluable. You are a treasure.

Nate Sewell was also introduced to me by Sandi Tompkins—another great gem and talent in the process. Thanks, Nate, for your diligent work to get this book to print, your awesome ability to listen well, to hear and see the vision for the cover nearly on the first attempt. You are amazing. And thanks also to Greg Burns, who generously offered his amazing photographs of the Carson Valley for me to choose from, and for Nate to have something to do his magic on!

Thanks to the three Burns women, Greg and Jeannie's beautiful daughters, Karen, Kris, and Alicia, for traveling these years with all of us. You were so young when this story began, but even then you unselfishly took Allie, Emma, and Rebecca into your hearts and lives those many months following Kurt's accident and for years to come. You became the best big sisters, the very best example for my girls. Like your mom, you have modeled well what generosity of heart looks like. You are truly family to us and so very loved.

To my dear friends, Carla, Carlee, Carllene, Celeste, Conny, Deb, Erin, Gloria, Karen, Lori, Marsha, Michelle, Peggy, Tracy, and my sister Chris, who have shared this journey with me over the years: a heartfelt thank you for your love and friendship.

Connie Marques, thank you for your wonderful counsel, shared wisdom, and for always pointing me to the Word—you have helped me through these many years with your sound advice, wise words, and encouragement. I appreciate and love you so much.

My life—our lives as a family—have been so blessed to call Lee and Audra Baumgarth our adopted parents, the girls' beloved "Papa" and "Nunie." Though Lee is now in Heaven, I want to thank you for taking us in as your own, unselfishly pouring into our lives for many years your love, guidance, support, and encouragement. Together, you have been an incredible example to us of a beautiful marriage founded solidly on your shared faith in Christ. Audra, Nunie, you are still beautiful inside and out at the wonderful age of 83! You are so very loved.

Jeannie Burns and Tina Smith, how can I even begin to thank these two women in my life? There are no words to describe all you have given me: the love, encouragement, strength, counsel, acts of service unending, and just being there for me in the darkest nights and through the longest journey.

Tina, thank you for journeying with me through life in most of these years, especially as our kids were growing up. Your quiet strength and help, your generous heart and wise words, have been a balm for my soul, and your friendship was a gift I couldn't have imagined when we moved to Smith Valley. You have stood with me, believing that I was to write even when the story had "died" and the initial manuscript sat in a box covered with dust . . . for years. You kept believing and let me know even when I thought there was nothing to say, nothing more to write, no story. You always believed that I was called to write. And, like my friend Karen said years ago, "I just believe, Shawn, that one day a book is going to come flying out of that box!" You believed. Thank you, my dear friend, for your faith and for your faithful friendship. You have been a great gift, and I love you so.

From the beginning, Jeannie, you arrived with the knock at the door that fateful Thanksgiving night just behind the paramedics, and you never lost step with me. You comforted me and kept me standing, cared for our little girls, and organized my world. You loved us through thick and thin, from the very beginning to the very end. Yes, this is the "greatest story of redemption and restoration," your very words to Kurt that last night—a story that you have been such an intricate and important part of, one which you really helped write. You have walked the miles and years with me, with Kurt and our girls, as my dear friend, confidant, and great treasure. There are no words to adequately thank you, but I pray that you know the great gift you have been in my life. You are God's great blessing, an angel without wings, one recognized as such by those who know you. You are a gift, a friend, truly a sister, who has blessed not only my life but the life of my family, my girls, far more than you will ever know. Thank you, Jeannie, for standing with me through life . . . always. You are so very loved.

For the many other family members, including my brother and sister-in-law, Mark and Trina Ward, my cousins Mike and Robin Bratton, and friends who have so generously helped us in so many ways, thank you. The journey would not have been possible without the help of so many. I am, truly, grateful.

Finally, to my three precious daughters: we have traveled these many years together, as a family weathering together the storms of life. Not easy at times, downright difficult at others, with rays of sunshine thankfully breaking through the darker clouds illuminating our way. Yes, once a family, always a family. Though we are far from perfect (an understatement, for sure!), the plans God has through all He allows are good. We may not see it in the midst of the storm, but one day, the storm will be stilled, and the rainbow appears. We see Him far more clearly now. You are all, each one, a unique gift, cherished and loved more than you know.

With love and thanksgiving,
Shawn Ward
November 2018

Author's Note

Tears stream down my cheeks as I sit to begin the writing down of this story—our story, but more truly, *His Story*. It's difficult to believe that this story is twenty years in the making: twenty very long years that somehow, in retrospect, have flown by. How can that be? But what are twenty years in light of eternity? This is a story about real life and real lives. Real life and eternity.

I feel a bit like Jo in *Little Women* when she finally heads to the attic to begin writing the "real" story, the one emblazoned deep in her heart, one that *had* to come forth from her pen, driven more by the heart than the head. I used to nearly cry when I watched her finally make her way to that treasured spot where much of life had happened for the March girls. Donned with cap and winter gown, she hid herself in the attic, surrounded by those things that still spoke much to her, with pen firmly in hand, dipping and drawing the words faithfully on the parchment paper.

Why such emotion, you ask? Tears like these came to me in the midst of the darkest years, years when my own story was lost (or so it seemed) in a storm too dark to describe, too severe perhaps to even survive. I wept with

Jo in the midst of life after my husband's near-fatal car accident, a traumatic brain injury, and long recovery. I wept tears of joy during the witnessing and blessing of many miracles—all with three little girls under four at the time. And I wept not many years later when our life was wreckage, darkness pulling us downward, life spiraling toward disaster. Sexual addiction and abuse . . . our marriage unraveling . . . .

As it all unfolded, I kept mounting those stairs to the attic with Jo. Every time she took up her pen, I wept. I knew one day I would tell the "real" story, as she did hers. But mine was so lost in hopelessness. What on earth could I write? Never did I think our marriage would go this way—but never did I expect the ending God had written.

For a time, it seemed that darkness had won. For a time. But God, the Eternal Chaser, never gives up. He never stops pursuing us. We may hide, but the Great Shepherd seeks us out, tenderly calling our name. He goes into our darkness to deliver us from our wilderness wanderings. The Great Lover of our soul beckons us to "Come!" and He patiently, passionately waits, His hand always extended to us.

A serious cancer diagnosis brought my former husband's and my life colliding back together again. Once a family, always a family: especially when you have kids. That summer, God wrote the end of the story . . . a story nearly unbelievable, but believable because He's God. He extended His hand of grace to my husband. His promise to me from eighteen years earlier came to fruition: *"Did I not tell you if you believe, you will see the glory of God?"*

And so, at long last, I enter into the attic myself, Jo-like. I only know that the story which was nearly forgotten, stored in a box for years, must be poured out now. The ending has been written. I share from our lives a journey: a powerful story of love and loss and devastation; one of hope and help, of joy and healing; a story of grief and sorrow, and ultimately, of redemption and restoration. Two fallible people, one broken marriage, and an infallible God whose desire is for us to turn to Him, no matter how broken, no matter how lost we may be.

I have struggled for quite some time to write the note to this book. How *much* do I share? The story is so big, God's weaving so intricate. *Exactly what* do I share? The details are so personal and so complicated; I don't want to offend anyone with them, and yet they are so important. Addiction, especially sexual addiction, is not a topic that many want to talk about, let alone face. Things like divorce, addiction, abuse, and unhealthy sexuality affect so many of us. In fact, we need to begin a "national conversation" about such things, if we are ever to face—

together, and with compassion—the battle that so many of us think we face alone. We must bring this taboo topic out from under the covers and into the light. Only when we do can the shame and the addiction be exposed for what they are—only then can repentance happen, the balm of love and grace pour forth, and the hard work of healing begin.

So, like Jo, I've finally put my pen to rest and gathered the stack of papers in my hands, wrapped a ribbon of raffia loosely around the precious book, and tucked a flower within the bow. This is my story, authentic and true, woven by God and forged through the years of life, both bitter and sweet—engraved on the tablet of my heart. I pour it out as an offering, vulnerable, but confident that God will use it for good. My desire is that you will find hope, courage, and grace as you read *HIS Story*. And my prayer is that you will reach out and take hold of the faithful hand of Jesus Christ, the One Who Knows All Things and who loves you like crazy.

Shawn Ward

~~~~~~~~~~~~~~~~~~~~~~~
Now to Him who is able
to do far more abundantly beyond all
that we ask or think,
according to the power that works within us,
to Him be glory in the church
and in Christ Jesus to all generations
forever and ever.
Amen.
Ephesians 3:20-21
~~~~~~~~~~~~~~~~~~~~~~~

Part One
The Beginning

— Chapter 1 —

In an Instant

I could hear Allie and Emma squeal in the living room as their daddy chased them, making his funny animal noises in pursuit of his two favorite subjects. Just three-and-a-half and barely two, the girls loved their daddy's attention. No matter how long his day or how tired he was, he never seemed to disappoint them. Tonight was no exception. He had tickled them nearly to tears and then turned into their favorite farm animals, chasing them wildly around the living room. My mom and I looked on with smiles on our faces. I had just finished nursing Rebecca, our one-month-old, when Kurt reached up his strong arms.

"This dad just needs to hold his baby." He slipped her onto his chest, rocking slightly to snuggle her close. Allie and Emma had grabbed a book and brought it to their dad for further entertainment—this was, once again, a typical night for us. Wild evenings full of laughter and lots of silliness.

It was a cold, clear Friday night after Thanksgiving, and we had spent the weekend and days prior moving into our rental home. This was our first night tucked into our new home, and we were glad to have time just to play with the girls and to visit with my mom.

Just a week before Rebecca's expected arrival, we accepted an offer on our home with a 45-day close, scheduled one day before Thanksgiving. Literally within a week of bringing our third baby home to her two expectant and adoring older sisters, we began to pack.

I must have been a bit crazy (or at least hormonal) when I agreed to such a "deal"—moving a full house and a construction business into a rental at the holiday time, with three babies under four. Kurt was so excited about moving toward our goal of building in Smith Valley. Carson Valley, at the eastern base of the great Sierra Nevada mountains, was growing rapidly, mainly due to the influx of retirees from California. Even though that was great for Kurt's booming construction business, he still wanted to move thirty minutes to this more rural valley. He had proposed this idea when we had first met six years earlier. For a city girl, my answer then was an unequivocal "No!"

But now, with friends and family leading the way and our family growing to five, I finally acquiesced. We had purchased the most beautiful property: ten acres nestled at the base of a great canyon, overlooking green farmland and the entire valley. The home we designed would be set among the pinion pines—the views, well, they were phenomenal. It seemed like a little slice of heaven.

Somehow, we made it—at least, we had our boxes moved into the new rental home, three babies and all. Yes, I do think we were crazy to try to accomplish such a task, but we could now settle in for the winter and continue with our plans to build and move.

Kurt had started the excavating for his shop and, as the weather permitted, we would continue the building process. I knew one thing for certain: Kurt would build our second home with the same quality and craftsmanship he had built many homes over the years. He was a perfectionist, an artisan builder, and a master craftsman. I was proud of my husband; we had become a good team in business and now wrestled with a busy life, full with three little blonde girls—babies, really—directing our lives. We were both excited about what lay ahead for us.

Since we hadn't been able to spend time with my mom on Thanksgiving Day, Kurt picked her up on this cold winter evening, along with dinner from our favorite Mexican restaurant. My mom was now in a convalescent home, as her health had continued to decline over the past seven years or more. Although she had not been formally diagnosed with a specific disease, she had a serious neurological disorder; she could hardly walk anymore and talking was becoming more and more difficult as well.

Her condition was so sad; it broke my heart to see her in such a state. But I know she enjoyed the time with us, seeing the girls, hearing their laughter. I was thankful for a husband who loved my mom and was kind and generous toward her. As I saw a slight smile on my mom's face and listened to the joyful noise in our chaotic home, I was grateful. Life was not perfect, but it was very, very good.

It was almost 7:45 when Kurt left to take my mom back home. As they put on their coats, Allie and Emmie insisted on hugging and re-hugging both Daddy and Grandma at the door. I kissed Kurt, as we always did when leaving, and hugged my frail mom. I assured her that we would see her again soon.

Towing the two older girls hand-in-hand down the hall, with little Rebecca in one arm, I got everyone ready for bed. Things were still unfamiliar for them in their new room, but we prayed as we usually did before bedtime and prayed specifically for daddy's safe return. The skies were clear, though the weather was frigid. After tucking Allie and Emmie into the same bed and kissing their sweet little faces, I put Rebecca in her infant seat and placed her on the countertop while I jumped into the shower. It had been a long, crazy, busy week with the move, Thanksgiving, the business, the babies, and my mom. I was glad the move was behind us.

When I got out of the shower, Rebecca had fallen asleep, so I gently laid her in her crib, which was in our bedroom, surrounded by stacks of boxes. As I jumped into my bed, I grabbed my Bible and began reading, but as I did, the words were swimming on the page. I thought about Kurt; he should be home by now. I prayed, "Lord, I hope Kurt is okay and that he'll be home soon."

Something happened then that never happened to me before or since. I saw a picture in my mind of three people lying in a field, covered with dark blue blankets. Above each of the bodies was a circle of light; two were up high, and one was low, hovering over the third body. I knew that these three people were Christians. "Lord," I whispered, "I pray that one of those three people is not Kurt. I pray that he is fine, that You would have mercy upon him and spare his life." And although I don't believe we can make deals with God, I prayed, "Lord, I'll go anywhere, do anything, give up anything, if You will spare his life."

Immediately, I shook off this "thought," as I didn't want to be a paranoid wife. Where could he be? He should have been home an hour or so ago now. Maybe he had to go buy something for my mom, or perhaps he stopped by a friend's or co-worker's house and forgot to mention to me that he was going to do so. I decided to wait ten more minutes, watching them tick by on the alarm clock by our bed.

Rebecca began to wake up and fuss a bit. Perhaps she was getting hungry. I picked her tiny body up, wrapped her snug in a blanket, and walked into the kitchen where our phone was. I began to call several people. Kurt had not taken his cell phone with him, so I couldn't try to call him directly. I first called the convalescent home. Yes, my mom was there and back in her room safely. When did she get back? The person on the phone thought it was about an hour or so ago. Where could Kurt be? I tried calling my brother to tell him about my concern, but when I called, his phone just kept ringing and ringing. No answer, no voicemail. Tried again. I then called a girlfriend. No answer. Left a message for her.

I snuggled Rebecca close to me and walked into the living room and up to the bay window looking outside. I saw three paramedics walking up the walkway, the ambulance silent in the background. I opened the door to meet them. Standing in the doorway in my flannel nightgown with Rebecca held close, the head paramedic said, "Hi, Shawn. My name is Dennis Atchison. I'm a friend of Kurt's. I'm sorry to tell you . . . There's been an accident."

Suddenly, the cold seemed to be ringing in my ears. Backing up with my hand covering my mouth, I weakly asked the only question that would come out: "How bad is it?"

Dennis replied, "Two people died, and they have care-flighted another person as well as Kurt to Reno, to Washoe Medical Center."

I knew at that moment, in an instant, life for us had changed.

Just then, my friend Jeannie came running up the walkway. "Shawn, it's gonna be okay. I'm here to drive you to Reno to the hospital." Jeannie had brought her mother-in-law, who was up visiting for the holidays, to stay with Allie and Emma.

The paramedics stepped inside, stating that, since care-flight could not transport two patients at the same time, they had taken Kurt mid-way to Reno by ambulance to Carson Tahoe Hospital in Carson City. Almost immediately upon their arrival at CTH, the care-flight helicopter landed, ready to transport Kurt on to Washoe Medical Center.

I went back to my bedroom, passing little Allie and Emma's room, quickly looking in to see if they were still asleep. They were. I hoped they would stay asleep. Jeannie and I went back to my room; I changed into some clothes and tried to gather the diaper bag and a few things. All three paramedics came in and asked, "Would you like to pray?" No words were spoken. Only a nod and all five of us hit the floor. I don't remember the prayers, but I remember the urgency of their words on behalf of Kurt and the other young man. I couldn't figure out how all these people got here, but I was thankful: for their presence, and for their prayers.

Suddenly the thought fleeted through my mind: how did the paramedics find us? As we headed to Reno, Jeannie—one of my best friends who had helped us with our recent move—explained how all the dots connected. Jeannie's husband, Greg, a volunteer firefighter in Gardnerville, responded to an emergency call: an auto accident at Highway 88 and Mottsville Lane, approximately five miles from their house. When he returned home, and she saw his face, she knew something was terribly wrong. "What? What?" she cried out. Greg replied, "It's Kurt, Kurt Rowlin . . . ."

As we drove on, Jeannie told me what Greg had quickly relayed to her about the accident. Three young people were in the other car. He thought two teenage girls had died (probably instantly) as their car had rolled at least once, and they were thrown from the vehicle. The other person was care-flighted from the scene. After the helicopter and ambulance left, Greg, the sheriffs, the NHP officers, and the other volunteers were inspecting the cars. When they looked inside the Honda Accord, they saw two baby seats strapped into the back seat. Opening the glove compartment, they found our registration. Greg was shocked. For a moment, there was panic and a hectic search to see if any little bodies could be found. Thankfully, Allie and Emmie were home tucked safely in bed.

As Jeannie talked, we would pray intermittently for Kurt and the other young man. I was a bit numb; the cars and lights seemed to be flashing by, but somehow our car seemed to be standing still. It seemed like it took forever to get to Washoe Medical Center.

Arriving at the emergency room, the receptionist began to ask me questions about insurance, contact information, etc. Her questions seemed to be unending. I wanted so to get in to see him. But the wait seemed way too long.

Jeannie continued to sit by me and comfort me with words of assurance, hugs, and her intermittent prayers. I was thankful she was there. What a friend she had been to me over the years—and now, well, she was God-sent.

As we waited, I remember looking at Rebecca's face, concentrating on each of her little features; I was so thankful for this little life. I smiled thinking how her big sisters had immediately begun to call her their "baby Becky." She was so tiny, just barely six pounds at five weeks old. Silently, I prayed fervently for her daddy. I tried not to think beyond that as we didn't know anything yet.

Finally, someone called my name, and I was allowed into the ER. The noisy room was a flurry of activity. Bright lights glaring down, Kurt was lying on a gurney in the center of the room—he wasn't even in his own cubicle or room yet. He was still in his jeans; his red chamois cloth shirt was torn or cut nearly off of his chest, his work boots still on his feet. There were cuts and dried blood on his face, forehead, chest, hands— his breathing seemed shallow. I thought his injuries didn't look *that* bad, but why wasn't he moving or responding to my words? "Please, Kurt! Please, God, let him hear me." I told him I loved him and that I needed him. As I kissed his ashen face. I told God that I loved Him and needed Him, too.

Soon, my brother Mark came into the ER and stood with me. He told me Trina, my sister-in-law, had gone to my house to stay with Allie and Emma. I was glad that they would wake up to Auntie and not a total stranger. As we stood there over Kurt, I remember

Mark praying over and over, through a breaking voice, "I just love this man, Lord. Please, show Yourself strong. Please, God, show Yourself strong." He repeated these words several times. As he prayed, I remember thinking, *That's a strange prayer, not really mentioning healing and saving Kurt.*

But as the words were repeated, I realized, *yes, God, we do need You to show Yourself strong.* Only God could help, heal, and save Kurt. We needed God to show Himself strong on all our behalf.

Lost in the moment, a nurse's gentle voice broke through: "We need to get Kurt in for an MRI and X-rays. You'll need to step back out into the waiting room."

"Yes, of course," I replied, though not really wanting to leave his side. The nurse could not make any comment on his condition at this point. He was unconscious, a probable head injury. Exactly what? We would have to wait.

As the doors swung open into the waiting room, there were many people already there, having somehow heard the news. There were probably ten or twelve people, including Dick Dankworth, a good friend of Lee and Audra's (our "adopted" parents who now lived in Kona, HI). "What are you doing here, Dick?" I was so surprised to see him.

"Lee sent me to see how you are doing if I could help." The compassion in his eyes spoke volumes to my heart. His big hug was somehow reassuring.

"How did Lee and Audra hear about the accident?" He didn't know, but having Dick there gave me a sense of comfort, almost like having a dad checking on me. Lee, or "Papa," as he was known to our girls, had sent his good friend to check on us and bring a father's comfort. The others being there made me feel like Kurt and I were loved.

We were such a large group that the receptionist moved us to a back room near the ICU to wait. I didn't want to fall apart, as we didn't know yet exactly what was wrong with Kurt, or even what was the extent of his injuries. Around midnight, I went to a quiet corner to nurse Rebecca. A few tears fell on her tiny cheek. She was surprised and started to fuss, but as I nuzzled into her precious little face, whispering, "It's okay, sweet baby girl," she was consoled. I didn't know if I was really telling her the truth. I so *wanted* it to be true. Like Becky, I too wanted to be consoled, for someone to tell me it was just going to be alright. My heart cried out silently to God.

Our group grew as we waited and seemed to keep on waiting. Kurt's best friends, Ray and Rob were there along with several subcontractors and other friends. We all must have felt time standing still. *Why haven't they come out to tell us yet of Kurt's condition?* It had been at least two hours. I suspected that the longer it took, the more serious the situation was.

When the doctor finally came out, the report was not good. "Kurt has suffered severe trauma to the brain, the left frontal lobe, a broken sternum . . . and other issues." I don't remember all that he said. The doctor stated that his injuries were very serious; he was not conscious at this point, and we would have to wait and see, especially with a traumatic brain injury. More tests needed to be done.

Ray asked the doctor, "Is it be possible that he might not make it?"

"Yes, it is possible, given his condition."

The room was perfectly quiet.

How could that be? Just a few hours ago, he was playing on the floor with our girls, making his funny animal sounds and reading them a book. Just a few hours ago, he was home with us—fit and strong and full of life. *How could that be?* The doctor's words nudged me painfully back to the present.

He indicated that very few visitors would be allowed to see Kurt in the ICU at this point and that those who did come in must be quiet, talking softly, as brain-injured patients could be agitated and disturbed by even a little noise. I didn't realize it then, but that was the first of many lessons on brain injuries that I and the rest of us would receive.

It was now about 2:00 a.m. Not much was said, but tears flowed from the eyes of others now in our small crowd. What do you say? We all prayed once again for Kurt and for God to spare his life and heal him. After a while, some people reluctantly left for home, many saying they would be back as soon as possible, some within hours. Others stayed on through the night and the next day and the day after. I was so thankful for these people, for friends and family that cared and loved us enough to be there.

Jeannie took little Rebecca so I could go back with Kurt. He was hooked up to so many machines and monitors; an oxygen mask covered most of his face. His body seemed so strong, yet lifeless at the same time. I talked to him as if he heard me, and when I couldn't talk, I prayed for my husband, trying to hold back the tears. Mark, my brother, came in to sit with me. For hours, we watched Kurt's chest rise and fall. It seemed almost mechanical, in sync with the beeping of the monitors. Doctors, nurses, and staff flurried in and out all the rest of the night, but I barely noticed.

Somehow, it was all so incongruous. Hours ago, we were home, together with our three little girls. Life was vibrant and full. Now, suddenly, it came to a halting STOP. Was this real? Could life change so fast?

Early that morning, I called Trina to check on Allie and Emma. At three-and-a-half and just two years old, they were both too little to understand what was going on. I reassured them that mommy would be home soon. I didn't know about their daddy. I was so thankful that Trina was with the girls. We decided that she would bring them up to see their baby sister and me the next day.

By early afternoon, the waiting room had many new faces. The look in each set of eyes again clearly revealed each one's love and concern for Kurt. Still, we didn't know much more than what the doctor had shared in the middle of the night.

Kurt's parents arrived with his brother, Matt, from the Sacramento area. Obviously distraught, they had a difficult time even approaching Kurt's bed. They stayed a little while and returned home. They would come back the next day, prepared to stay for a few days. Unable to acknowledge even their presence, only tears were shed when his sister and brother-in-law stood silently by Kurt. There were no words. My heart broke for them all.

Jeannie began to schedule many of our women friends to come to the hospital, taking shifts to hold and care for Rebecca so I could be with Kurt, free to meet with doctors while still being able to nurse her. For now, Jeannie stayed with me. I couldn't ask for a better friend, who would become to me more like the dearest of sisters. I didn't yet know how much I would need her and others who already were standing at our side.

Others' outpouring of help began that first day. Rob and Ray would contact current job subcontractors and homeowners, notifying them of the situation. They would keep the jobs going until Kurt got back to work. Kurt was a master craftsman, building some of the most beautiful, custom homes in the area. They would be the gate-keepers for Kurt, standing watch, completing what needed to be done in a manner that Kurt himself would approve.

Soon, we learned that the driver of the other car was a twenty-year-old young man living in San Diego. He was from Indonesia. We didn't have any information yet about the cause of the accident, other than that the two cars collided at the intersection of Highway 88 and Mottsville Road, only a few miles from town.

During that first day, I began to have these words repeatedly come to my mind: *"'For I know the plans I have for you,' declares the LORD, 'plans to prosper you and not to harm you, to give you hope and a future.'"* I didn't know exactly what scripture this was, but it just kept coming back to my thoughts again and again. I finally asked someone where that verse was in the Bible—Jeremiah 29:11 (NIV). I felt encouraged; perhaps God was saying to my heart, "I am going to heal Kurt. He's going to recover." You don't give hope or a future to a dead person. I truly wanted to believe this was a word specifically for Kurt.

Kurt did not respond to conversation, stimulus, or even pain during those first days. A squeeze of his hand. *Nothing.* A pinch on his shoulder by the doctor. *Nothing.* An "I love you." *Nothing.*

Mid-afternoon on Sunday, our "adopted" parents, Lee and Audra, flew in from Hawaii. Wheeling Audra's wheelchair into the room, they greeted Kurt. He immediately responded, "Hi, Lee!" We were all so excited and encouraged, thinking that this might be the beginning of him "coming around." Even the doctors seemed encouraged.

I was so happy and relieved to see Lee and Audra. They really were like parents to us, and especially to me, since my own parents were not actively involved in our lives.

We had spent a lot of time with them over the years, and they were truly family to us. Kurt had done the finish work on their beautiful Victorian home in Genoa when we first met. Then we lived with them for several months while we finished building our new home, around the time Allie was born. Little Allie came "home" to her first home at Lee and Audra's. Allie would push Audra in her wheelchair and when she was very little, she would say, "Nun, nun, nunnie!" over and over. Thus, Audra became 'Nunie' and Lee, their beloved 'Papa.'

This was the first time for them to see Rebecca. Lee, coming up behind me as I unwrapped her from her pink blanket, exclaimed, "Wow, she really is beautiful!" All three of the girls looked like Precious Moments babies, all three darling blondes. Unfortunately, Lee and Audra only stayed for two days before they were called to Boston. Their own son was critically ill with cancer, so they needed to be with him. It was difficult to see them grieve the possible loss of two sons: one biological and dearly loved; one "adopted" and dearly loved.

More and more people flooded the ICU waiting room. Many of the men who wanted to see Kurt began to volunteer to take shifts to stay with him through the night. We had a Bible by the bed, and we encouraged people to read and talk quietly to Kurt. I really felt in my heart that he might be able to hear, even though he wasn't responding outwardly.

On the fourth day, the doctors began giving me information on brain injury. I didn't bother to read it then, as I wanted to believe that Kurt was going to be healed. Jeremiah 29:11 continued to roll through my mind.

By then, we learned that the ICU doctors had been in contact with the young driver's family in Indonesia and that they were trying to decide whether to leave him on life support or not. Apparently, there was very little brain activity. With the difficulties of the distance, language, and the grievous situation they faced with their son in such a tragic state so far from them, it took several days. They finally decided to take him off life support. Within hours, he passed away. I felt so incredibly grieved for them and could only imagine their pain and sorrow.

Almost immediately after learning of his passing, I knew in my heart: He, this young man, was the third one. In my vision—as I now knew it to be called—there were three people, and he was the third and last one. I felt assured that Kurt would live, that God would spare his life.

In those first days and weeks, there was an incredible outpouring of people who came into our lives to help and to pray. Many were our old friends, people we had known and loved; others were brand new.

Tara, our friend who was talking with Jeannie when they learned of the accident, started the prayer chain at our church. The word spread throughout our valley and surrounding areas, other churches committing to pray. Lee and Audra worked with YWAM, a Christian missionary organization serving all over the world, and they began notifying friends and family. Lee made up 24-hour prayer sign-up sheets distributed to local churches, some nearly a hundred miles away, for anyone who would commit to pray for Kurt and our family for an hour out of each and every day. Amazing to think that there were people, many whom we did not know, up at all hours night and day, who would faithfully pray to God for Kurt's healing and recovery. Literally, hundreds of people were now praying for Kurt. Heaven was being bombarded.

— Chapter 2 —

The Wait

I turned over early one December morning, pulling up the covers. It felt so cold. The temperatures had been dropping down into the teens all week, and it had snowed on the way home from the hospital. Looking at the messy bed, there were two little lumps snuggled under the covers. *How did we all get in here?* I thought.

It was my first night back home, and I had picked up Allie and Emma at Jeannie's around 6:30. The girls had insisted that I sleep with them in their bed. At some point last night, I must have made my way back to our bed for some more comfortable sleep, and Allie and Emmie had followed me. I hadn't even heard them, which concerned me a bit. Then, realizing Rebecca hadn't fussed during the night and so hadn't been nursed, I quickly went over to her crib to check on her. She was sleeping so peacefully I decided not to change her. Relieved, I got back quietly into bed for some much-needed rest. It was barely light, and I was hoping everyone would sleep for a while longer.

As I dozed off, I could hear a strange clattering sound outside. I couldn't make it out at first. Listening intently, I finally realized it was the sound of scraping and shoveling. Someone had arrived at the very break of dawn to shovel the snow and ice off our walks and driveway. I couldn't believe it! I thought it would be nice to greet our unannounced but welcomed helper with a cup of hot coffee. But before I thought again, I was sound asleep.

I never found out who our unidentified "shoveler" was that winter morning. No one seemed to know. We were receiving help in so many ways, from so many. A friend had rented me a car since ours was totaled in the accident. Someone else gave me a cell phone, and another person, who wanted to remain anonymous, paid for the cell phone service. When we arrived home that first night, there was dinner, dessert, and fresh flowers on the table. That was just one of many such blessings. I felt surrounded by love and knew we were being taking care of by hands we often could not see.

One of the first nights in the ICU, I was by Kurt's bedside. It was late, around 11:00 p.m. So many people had made their way past the nurses to see Kurt, and since everyone had been so good about keeping the rules, being polite, and being quiet, they relaxed the "few visitors" rule for us. I was thankful. When I saw someone sneak in this late night, I realized it was my dear friend, Cyndi.

"What are you doing here?" I whispered. She and her husband, Phil, had moved with their four children to manage a Young Life camp about an hour out of San Diego several years earlier.

"When we heard about the accident, I couldn't stand not being here with you, knowing you had all three of your little girls!" We hugged until we cried. She stayed through the night with me in the ICU. Others would do the same.

The days and nights in the ICU were difficult, but I was thankful that we had been prepared in some ways. Just about a year before the accident, we had gone to Hawaii to see Lee and Audra. We planned to leave two-year-old Allie and ten-month-old Emmie with them for two nights to attend a concert. Life was so very busy day-to-day, and this was our chance to have a real date—our first extended date since the first two girls had come into our world.

This made us realize it was time to get our affairs in order. I had attended a Christian Financial Concepts training course and had become a financial counselor. Our need for a trust, power of attorney, and the like was apparent. We were young, and the chances of something happening seemed remote, but we certainly wanted to know if something did happen that we would have directives for the care of our two little girls. In getting our trust, it was easy for us to complete the power of attorney, physicians' directives, and other important documents. Somehow, even in this, God had prepared us in a way. I was able now to make all of Kurt's decisions: business, personal, and medical.

Kurt was still in a coma after being in the ICU for over a week. Concerned, the doctors had more MRIs, scans, and testing done. After he responded to Lee and Audra, we were all hopeful that he would regain consciousness and his recovery would begin.

Rushing into the room to meet with the neurologist, Dr. Johnson, I saw that he now had the test results in his hands and was ready to see me. He motioned for me to sit in the chair by Kurt's bed.

"We thought, initially, that Kurt would be responding, improving better than he has by now," he said. "From these recent scans, we've learned that there is greater injury to his brain than we knew at first."

I waited, silent.

Looking down initially and not directly at me, Dr. Johnson continued, "Kurt not only suffered a severe injury to the left frontal lobe of his brain, but he also has a brain stem injury." He didn't say any more.

'What does that mean?' I asked, staring at him.

"Well . . ." He seemed to hesitate, choosing his words carefully. "It probably means a longer, more difficult recovery."

"Will he get better? Will he recover, do you think?"

"I don't know. There is no way to know. We will just have to wait." He went on to say that the longer Kurt remained in the coma, the less likely he would come out of it without some permanent damage. My head swirled with the news.

Time was important. Did the doctor believe that he *would* come out of the coma? He wanted to offer hope, but at that point, no one really knew. He indicated then that I might expect a "changed" Kurt, even if he did come out of the coma. His personality could likely be different.

I remember praying and asking the Lord to please not let him be child-like. I had three little babies now and couldn't handle Kurt being anything less than himself. *Please, Lord, let him have his same personality, let him be an adult, fully himself.* This was the cry of my heart that day and for many days following.

Shortly after this, Kurt was transferred to the neurology floor, as he was in "stable" condition. A GI doctor performed a procedure to insert a G-tube into his abdomen so that he could get the nutrition he needed.

Faithful men continued to come to stay with him through the nights, reading, talking quietly to him, praying. It was amazing to see some of these big, burly men come in at night after a long day's work and want to be there, want to help, want to spend time by Kurt's bedside. I imagine that all of them prayed for Kurt, even if they weren't believers. Who else do you turn to in a crisis like this? Only God can heal such an injury, bring someone from the depths of a coma and back to life, to health again. Only God.

During this time, our friend, Dr. James Golden, a retired neurosurgeon from Stanford, was coming into the hospital to check on Kurt. Kurt had built a home for him and his wife when they retired to the Carson Valley. Jim had talked to the doctors while visiting us at the hospital. I didn't know it then, but by the third week or so after Kurt's accident, he didn't have much hope that Kurt would ever recover.

One morning, I left extra early to spend the day with Kurt. Jeannie came and picked up Allie and Emma. My friend Peggy met me at Starbucks in the hospital lounge area. Later, my friend Gloria would come in, along with her husband, John, who came nearly every day to see Kurt and to be with me. So many of my friends continued to volunteer six to eight hours each day to watch little Becky, taking shifts to cover the long days.

As I sank into the big chair next to Kurt's bed, hazelnut Americano in hand, I put my books on the table. I wished that he would wake up to have a cup of coffee with me and talk to me. "Good morning, Kurt!" I said. I didn't expect a response and didn't get one. I thought how handsome he still was.

We had been introduced through my brother and sister-in-law six years ago. I was living in Sacramento after my graduation from U.C., Berkeley, Haas School of Business. I considered myself a "city girl," having lived and worked in the city for quite some time. Kurt . . . well, he was certainly more of a country boy. He had graduated from U.C., Davis with a degree in Wildlife & Fisheries Biology, and he quickly made his way back to the Sierra Nevada Mountains, initially as a fire-fighter and forester, and later becoming a general building contractor.

Kurt introduced himself to me initially via letter. In fact, we wrote back and forth for weeks before actually meeting in person. It was what he told me in one of those first letters that now brought a smile to my face once again. In describing himself, he told me that he loved hiking and fishing, cross-country skiing, the outdoors, and nature. He loved his work, but the business side of his construction company could use some help (I think he was hinting!). But what really made me laugh then is that, when he described himself physically, he said, "Well, some people think I look a little like Robert Redford . . . only taller."

I didn't fully understand his dry sense of humor then but knowing it now so well, I smiled, thinking to myself, *Yes, he is that handsome; and really, he does look a bit like Robert Redford!*

So much life had happened for us in those six short years. We met and got married nine months later in September 1987. Two and a half years after that, we had our first daughter, our first miracle, Allie Krisean. Emma Noel, our second precious daughter, was born twenty months later. Rebecca Nicole arrived exactly two years after Emma, right on time. We were blessed with three precious baby girls within three and a half years.

I glanced over at Kurt from where I sat beside his bed. Bringing our little Rebecca home just seven weeks ago, I had felt that life could not be fuller or any more blessed than it was. Life seemed nearly perfect. Then. Just seven weeks ago.

Sometimes, things come crashing into our lives: unexpected things that turn our entire world upside down and sideways. They threaten to throw us off-course, destroy our foundation, and even wreck our faith.

But *God*.

Though I cried at Kurt's bedside that morning, I remembered God and His words in Jeremiah 29:11. Whatever His plan, somehow it would be for good. I needed His help to believe.

Another week in the neurology unit, and Kurt had not improved. Doctors and insurance decided it was time to move him to a rehab center. He was "stable" and ready for rehab, they said. But he wasn't even opening his eyes much; how could he be going to a rehab facility? How do you rehabilitate someone who is not responding? I'll never forget the day our friend Nate had come to tell me that Kurt was "up": in a wheelchair. I remember the shock of seeing Kurt strapped to the back of the chair, his head hanging limply forward, his hair covering his face. *That's not my husband!* I cried silently to myself.

When we checked into the rehab center, immediately the admitting nurse mentioned that I should get to know another young wife whose husband had experienced a traumatic brain injury. It would be good for us to get to know one another, as we had a lot in common with our husbands and our situations.

Her husband, Jason, had already been in rehab for over five weeks and was not making much—if any—progress. Although he was conscious, it seemed still that he was not cognitively aware of his surroundings, even of his young wife's presence and constant attempts to talk with him, to engage him. Within a week of our arrival, doctors decided that Jason was not suited for rehab, and they would need to find a long-term care facility for him. The only place that would take him at the age of twenty-nine in the nearest four or five states was a facility in Arizona. I remember being so upset that they had "given up" on Jason. It made me wonder for just a moment if the same thing might happen to my husband. But I had those words of hope from Jeremiah 29:11, the vision, and the belief that God was going to heal Kurt. I believed he was going to recover, and so did so many others.

But there were times, especially after Kurt went into rehab, that my faith faltered. When the PTs propped Kurt up to sit on a bench, he would wobble for a few seconds, then flop over on the long, padded bench. They would repeat the "exercise" over and over. He looked like a limp rag doll falling helplessly down. I felt as though I needed to go rescue him. *That's my husband,* I thought. Sometimes I had to leave the room.

Other times, watching the PTs put Kurt in a sling-like contraption was nearly as difficult to watch. The therapists would hoist him into a standing position with the support of the sling, then let the tension slacken. Kurt's legs would immediately shake like crazy, now unable to bear the weight of his own thin body. He had lost 45-50 pounds. He had become so skinny, so weak. The strong, hard-working, athletic husband I knew couldn't even stand up on his own two feet. It was heart-wrenching.

We were nearing the holidays. I so love Christmas, everything about it. The miracle of Christ born as a babe, the Son of God coming into the world to save us. His gift of grace. Our need for such grace. This year, we needed His grace in a different way: we needed a miracle. Kurt had remained in a coma for more than four weeks at this point.

God, Emmanuel. Heal Kurt. I knew that many were praying as fervently as I was.

Though it didn't feel like Christmas, I'll never forget coming home to lights strung on our home and on the tree in the yard—*how'd they get there? Who put them up? How did they know I love Christmas lights?* Again, unseen hands and hearts that kept on giving gave me a sense of comfort that even today I can't begin to express.

Just days before Christmas, I was finally home for the entire night with the girls. A knock came at the door. As I opened it, five men bounded in—grown men, not elves—carrying teddy bears, dolls, stockings stuffed with delightful things. Two of the men were paramedics, one involved the night of the accident; three were men who worked in the building trades—big men with big hearts.

Nearly speechless, I started to thank them, but one man—Kurt's good friend and co-worker, 'Little' Ray—stopped me and said, "Wait. There's more." He began to pull a huge stack of bills from his jeans pocket. I was speechless. I didn't have any idea how much money was in that pile, but that didn't matter one bit. The thought was what counted. The love was what counted, and that was immeasurable.

'Little' Ray, a confirmed bachelor who had worked with Kurt now five years or so, started to tell me that the money was collected for Kurt. "We, well, we started . . ." he said, his voice halting. He lowered his head; his hands shook. He loved Kurt and was devastated over his condition.

Robert stepped up. "Ray has been going into the local pubs and bars over the past three weeks, letting people know that there was a 'Kurt Rowlin' fund for those who wanted to help, to give." Ray humbly turned away, not wanting any recognition. I hugged them; they hugged me, too. I couldn't keep the tears back. Most of these big men were fighting back tears as well.

These special men came bearing gifts as if for a king, for royalty. I felt as if we had been served by the greatest of people. When they left, I looked at each gift, each package, and was overwhelmed by people's thoughtfulness and generosity. In that pile of bills, there was over $5,000—given to us in our time of need, this time of uncertainty and grief. I had not even thought about Christmas shopping, not even for our three little girls. It was okay. Someone else had. We were taken care of.

Despite the grief and sadness of the time—the wondering whether, in fact, Kurt would be healed—many loving, generous, and kind people had made our load much lighter. Another account was opened at Bank of America in Kurt's name, and funds started coming into that account from anyone who felt led to give. Over the course of the next few weeks, more than

$8,000 was deposited for our use: for medical bills, or whatever else was needed for us and our young family.

The thoughtfulness and generosity stretched beyond what this pen could ever record. There was a local contractor who even hired Kurt's crew to frame a custom home to keep them busy, provide them with work, during these winter holiday months. Then he gave the profits from the job to Kurt and me. Unbelievably generous. Unbelievably kind. How could we ever thank so many gracious people?

Jeannie came to take care of Rebecca for the night, in the midst of all this. She told me of an idea she had: when Kurt comes home, we should have a huge thank-you dinner for everyone who had helped us. I couldn't believe it; I'd been thinking the same thing earlier that day. In the next week, both my brother and our friend John Burruel approached me with the same idea. It felt like such a God-thing, His guidance even in the small details.

The help and kindness of so many continued day after day, week after week, and even over the many months to lighten our load, to lift our burdens through a time when it would have been impossible to go it alone. I was overwhelmed and so grateful for the "many" who helped us so much.

Kurt was now saying a few words at times. One night, the nurses had strapped his wrists to the bed to make sure he didn't get up. Kurt did not like that at all, and he made it clear. I felt sorry for our young friend Joe who had sat with Kurt through the night. He looked tired, and I knew the night was a hard one.

Kurt was now able to get into the shower with the help of an OT, and he could shuffle himself a short distance sitting up in a wheelchair. He was making improvements: little ones. But not much, it seemed. How could it be almost Christmas? I had believed Kurt would be home with us by now.

Then on December 21st, Kurt took his first few steps on his own toward the bathroom. It seemed monumental!

The next day, my friend Marsha, a nurse, called from Nashville, telling me how concerned she and her husband (a doctor at Vanderbilt) had been that Kurt was not improving.

Out of her concern, she had called an elderly friend in Wisconsin, Alice Campbell, to pray for Kurt. When Alice asked what had happened to Kurt, Marsha told her about the accident, his head injury and brain stem injury. Alice said, "Oh, perhaps we should ask the Lord to take him home to heaven!"

"Alice, we can't! He has three little baby girls. God has to heal him!"

"Then let's pray," Alice declared.

Marsha conveyed to me how fervently this aged but feisty woman had approached the throne of God, with such tenacity in her prayer request to God: "I felt like we were rushed directly into the throne room of God. I have never heard anyone pray like that before! Tell me, Shawn: did anything happen yesterday with Kurt?"

I felt elated. "Marsha, Kurt took his very first steps on his own yesterday afternoon!" God had answered Alice's fervent prayer. I asked Marsha to thank Mrs. Campbell for praying, and I begged her to continue. It was then that Marsha told me that Alice had lost her only son years ago in a car accident, and because of that, she felt called to pray for others who were suffering. She knew the pain of loss. She also knew the power of fervent and effective prayer. God had answered the faithful prayers of this sweet little woman in Wisconsin.

It was Christmas Eve. Mark and Trina took Allie and Emma so they could be with their older cousins, Gavin and Natalie, and I could go see Kurt for a few hours. Carrying Rebecca in my arms, I didn't find Kurt in his room. As we approached the nurses' station, Kurt was there slouched in his wheelchair. He began murmuring, trying to tell me something.

He kept repeating to me a word that sounded like "Blind, blind." I knew that he could see me, but I couldn't understand what he was trying to tell me. Then he said several times, "Six, seven. Six, seven." I couldn't for the life of me figure out what he was trying to say. He seemed frustrated. He repeated the words again.

"Kurt, you're not blind." I knew he could see me. It was so heart-breaking not to be able to understand what he was saying or to communicate with him or help him. It was such a grief to see him there on Christmas slumped in a wheelchair, and then to leave him behind. It just wasn't right. How could this be Christmas? It didn't seem like it. At least not in my heart.

After Christmas, I called Dr. Hershewe, a neuro-ophthalmologist, as I had started to be concerned that perhaps Kurt was really telling me he couldn't see. When Dr. Hershewe came to the rehab, I know he was visibly moved when he saw all three of our little girls there in the room, Allie and Emmie sitting on the bed with their daddy, Becky in my arms. After an attempt to communicate with Kurt about his vision, it was clear: he would not be able to do any kind of testing until Kurt was "further along" and able to respond to the questions and eye tests.

My heart sank. I thought that I could at least help Kurt in this way. Instead, I had to wait.

Seemed like we'd been waiting so long.

— Chapter 3 —

Miracles Beyond Measure

From the beginning, I felt a prompting to record the many miracles and good things that the Lord was doing: the vision, the hope through scripture that the Lord had given me in Jeremiah 29:11, the blessings we had received through the many acts of kindness from so many, the words of hope, prayers of life and encouragement that were poured over us daily.

About three weeks after the accident, a man came into Mark's business, talking about the accident and asking if we had received the police report yet. We had expected to receive it by now, but for some reason, it was delayed. We still didn't know the reason for the accident: only that it looked like the other car had run the stop sign entering the highway, the two cars colliding. But we didn't know anything for sure.

Mark told the man that, no, we hadn't received the report. The man then asked Mark if we knew if there was alcohol involved; Mark said no, he didn't think so, but again, we wouldn't know for sure until we received the Nevada Highway Patrol report. This man was Mark's brother-in-law's father. He didn't think that there would be evidence of alcohol found: his neighbor had been neighbors at one time of the family of the girls who had died, and they had never known the girls to be given to drinking.

Weeks after my friend Cyndi had walked into the ICU room that late night, I learned another piece of the puzzle. Cyndi had gone back to the Young Life camp near San Diego after seeing us. About two weeks later, she and Phil had asked an elderly man who volunteered once a week at the camp to pray for their friend Kurt in Carson Valley, who had been in a car accident at Thanksgiving.

The elderly man looked at them and said, "Our church in San Diego just had a memorial service for those three kids." He'd been praying for Kurt even though he didn't know his name! What an amazing thing: God seemed to be connecting the dots from my vision to the strong possibility of these kids' faith. I was so thankful for that knowledge and the peace that came with it for me, believing they had indeed gone to heaven. I wrote this down in my journal. Many of us continued to pray for the two families who had lost their children. I could only imagine the heartache and grief they were enduring.

Despite the moments of sadness, there was much to be thankful for; Kurt was alive, and I still believed that God was going to heal him. I remembered Jeremiah 29:11 and thanked God for the hope and future that I believed He had for Kurt. Many others believed that, too. Dozens and dozens of people from the very beginning shared their belief that God was going to heal him completely. There were so many still praying for Kurt. They hadn't given up either and continued to faithfully stand in the gap.

Jeannie and her girls continued to have Allie and Emma every day so that they would not be bounced around. Jeannie's daughters Karen and Kris (the twins), and her youngest daughter, Alicia, became like the best big sisters anyone could ask for, playing with the girls for hours on end, taking them to their high school basketball games and events . . . Allie and Emmie were like little appendages to the girls' sides. They were with Jeannie during the days, and then the Burns girls would pour into their little lives throughout the afternoons and evenings.

It would be a life-long love and respect for these older, selfless girls and their precious mom who served them—who served us all for many, many months. This family graciously gave and kept on giving into our lives. They became our closest "family" and really helped shape my girls into the young women they would become. Sometimes we don't realize the effect that we have on the lives of others, but I can now attest to the powerful influence that the four Burns girls, all women now, have had on my three daughters. In many ways, my girls are who they are because of having lived with and spent long days, many months and years, around a family that wouldn't let us go, who set their compasses due north in serving us. And we—yes, we— were all changed, blessed beyond measure by their pouring into our lives.

Many other people, near and as far away as Australia, continued to be there for us in various ways. Some people come into our lives for a day, a few months, or a season, and some come into our hearts and lives never leaving, never giving up, always giving. We were incredibly blessed to have had such people in our lives. They made our load lighter, giving graciously, generously, unreservedly. Their deeds are eternally recorded by the One who sees everything. For me, I know I will never forget their gracious gifts of help and hope, encouragement and love.

The paramedics, and dozens of others each week continued to come and see Kurt in rehab. One morning, the paramedic Ralph Jones came, and we visited in the front lobby. He began to talk about the night of the accident. After taking Kurt to meet care-flight at Carson Tahoe Hospital, Dennis mentioned wanting to come and tell me the news directly. They began to pray that they wouldn't get another call. Not many people knew that we had just moved, so it was amazing to learn how they "found" our house that night.

Ralph had called Kurt's electrical subcontractor, Rick, whom I had seen the day we moved our household goods. Rick described the rental house since he had met with Kurt's client, our landlord, prior to her moving to her new home. He didn't know the address but only the general vicinity and remarked that it had a bay window in front and was on the corner of a cul-de-sac facing south. By Rick's description, Ralph thought he knew that house; he had done electrical work on the side years back, and this house was familiar to him! Amazing. And they didn't even receive another call. I was thankful they were the ones to deliver the news that night, who came in to pray with Jeannie and me.

The New Year came, and still no real significant progress cognitively for Kurt.

On the morning of January 6th, I walked into Kurt's room expecting to see him sitting and staring rather blankly or sleeping in a curled heap. Instead, he was lying on his side, propped up on his left elbow. "What am I doing here?" he said, as I stared, astonished. "Was I in an accident or something?"

His questions were as direct and intentional as any he had ever asked me, and the look in his deep blue eyes was anything but a blank or a disengaged stare. Kurt was back! It was him! Kurt, my Kurt, *our* Kurt—and he was talking as if he hadn't missed a day! It truly was a miracle. He had fully come out of the comatose state and was himself. God had even answered that prayer just for me.

He began to quiz me on what had happened to him. As I answered his questions, I asked, did he remember any of it? No, not even Thanksgiving or dinner with my mom. He asked about Allie and Emma, but when I mentioned Rebecca, he didn't remember that we had had a third baby girl. As we talked, he then remembered me being pregnant but nothing about Rebecca's birth. Part of his memory—his more recent memory—was gone. But as we talked, it was evident that he knew some things and issues about people during these past weeks.

He talked about his friend Allen, a hard-driven type-A businessman in the construction industry, who had wept over Kurt at his bedside. "Boy, hasn't Allen changed," he said. Allen had been one who stayed by Kurt's bedside many nights even reading him the Bible. I remember Allen telling me one day after spending the night with Kurt in his rehab room that he now "understood why we are to work just six days." He said, "Because God rested on the seventh day!"

Then regarding another friend, Vic, a talented draftsman but a little rough around the edges at times: "He certainly has softened," Kurt observed. It was Vic who had lovingly brought in a final draft of our new house plans while Kurt was in the ICU—he must have stayed up for several nights in a row to complete them. He was also one who stayed nights by Kurt's bedside.

Then Kurt asked me, "Who's been ministering to you?" Not exactly the words he might have used in the past. Well, I had so much to tell him. I tried to gather my thoughts, all my thoughts, in those few moments. How could I possibly sum it all up? Just then I saw a card that someone had sent to us weeks earlier on the table next to Kurt's bed. I said, "Listen, I'll tell you . . ."

I read to him the entire poem, "Footprints" by Margaret Fishback Powers. God had been carrying me. I tried not to cry as I read it. I couldn't believe that Kurt was awake, talking and listening. He then said, "I'm so glad. I was worried about you." He kissed my forehead. I kissed his lips; he kissed me back.

How could I tell him all that had happened? I told him only a little of the accident, as I didn't want to overwhelm him. I did tell him, "There have been hundreds and hundreds of people who have been praying for you, Kurt."

"I know. I've felt it," he replied emphatically.

Amazing. Yes, amazing. How did Kurt know these things? He was more aware than we knew, sensing and hearing things, even though he couldn't respond. We do not always know what someone in a coma or with a debilitating disease that affects their mental capabilities knows, hears, or observes even while seeming disconnected from the world around them.

Kurt was proof of that. I marveled during our conversation that day.

I couldn't believe my eyes, my ears. To see and hear my husband who seemed near death come back to this state—it was unbelievable. I made calls to Jeannie, Mark, Lee and Audra, family members, and others who began to spread the good—no, the great news: *God had miraculously healed Kurt!* Yes, He had answered our zillion prayers! Kurt was awake, wide awake. And he was the same Kurt we all knew and loved.

That very day, Kurt was scheduled to have the G-tube removed from his stomach. They transferred us to Washoe Med by ambulance. I will never forget Dr. Harrison seeing Kurt. He seemed a little confused but didn't say much. Kurt and I continued to chat away as he was in the corner of the room looking at his notes. When he finally spoke, he said he could hardly believe it was Kurt, given Kurt's condition when he first inserted the feeding tube over a month ago. It was like a miracle. Oh, yes, it was, and I told him about the prayers of so many and how God had faithfully answered.

Many people came in to see Kurt in the next days, including the paramedics. It was then that Dennis told me how worried he had been after the doctors had told us Kurt also had a brain stem injury. Dennis shared with me the story of one patient with a supposed head injury. He was doing well in the ambulance: his vitals were strong, breathing was good, and all of a sudden, he was gone. Dennis and the rest of the medics were so upset, shaken, and perplexed as to why this man had died so unexpectedly, so suddenly.

They found out later: he had a brain stem injury. That's what happens as the brain stem swells and comes through the base of the skull, resulting in instant death. Or, if a patient with a brain stem injury does live, they are often left in a vegetative state. I was so thankful that I didn't know this before Kurt had come out of his coma and was in such a good place. Even in this God protected me. Thankfully, His plan for Kurt was not the "normal." His plan was for good— He had brought Kurt back from a very grave place.

Later, I learned that a woman, Leslie from Smith Valley who knew my brother and his family, had been praying faithfully for Kurt and for us these past six weeks. Although they didn't know us, like many people who felt great compassion and a passion to pray for Kurt, they came into our lives to help us, to join hands with us, really to bow down before a great God. They were there to help me, to lift our hearts and hands to a God who sees all things, knows all things: a God who hears our prayers.

Leslie was one of the many people who had signed up to pray for a specific hour each day. Her "time slot," her prayer hour for Kurt, was 3:00 a.m. on her church's prayer sign-up sheet. Only the called, the ones who know to Whom they are praying—to the only One who can help us in our time of such great need—would get up in the middle of the night, night after long night, to make their requests known to Him.

In the first days after the accident, Leslie and other women prayed for everything from Kurt's brain to his broken sternum. I too had been praying for every body part that I could name during those long hours in ICU.

Days later, while I was in the room, the doctor examining him (while reviewing Kurt's file and training several young medical residents) mentioned that Kurt had a broken sternum. He placed his palm on Kurt's chest, gently pushing in. He looked a little confused and said, "I don't believe this patient has a broken sternum." He mentioned that if he did, Kurt would most likely have contusions (bruising) on his chest. He read the notes again and, in a stern tone, told the young doctors how important it was to record things factually.

"Did this man," he asked, "really have a broken sternum or not? Were there X-rays or scans that support this diagnosis?" No one said a thing. Who knows whether Kurt's sternum was fractured, or whether God had healed him? It didn't matter: Kurt did not, now, have a broken sternum. Our specific prayers were answered.

In those initial weeks, Leslie was praying one early morning after Kurt's accident when she saw a picture of Kurt being healed, coming out of the coma, and talking to me directly, fully awake, fully restored. He told me that he loved me. Now, many weeks later, that vision had come to fruition. Kurt was wide awake and healed!

Leslie would be Allie's kindergarten teacher a year and a half later when we finally moved to Smith Valley. It's amazing how God brings people into our lives for such a time as this. God is moved by the prayers of the saints. I knew in my heart He had heard our cries on Kurt's behalf. He had spared Kurt's life. I knew it. He knew it. We all knew it.

Now that he could communicate, Kurt told me that he couldn't see well, that his vision had, in fact, changed. Dr. Hershewe, the neuro-ophthalmologist, returned to rehab to test Kurt's vision. This time, Kurt could fully articulate what he was seeing. Through testing, Dr. Hershewe discovered that he had what is called excyclotorsion. Due to the impact and the force of the collision, his eyes had literally rotated in their sockets, causing his vision to be severely impaired.

When Kurt had been saying to me, "Blind, blind . . . six, seven," he was actually trying to communicate that he literally saw multiple images, something like looking through a kaleidoscope, Dr. Hershewe informed us. He knew he couldn't see; he just couldn't articulate it. Now he could. The doctor was again moved: this time at the "miracle" he had seen in Kurt's recovery. He didn't even charge us for the appointment.

Kurt got an eye patch to alleviate some of the multiple images and dizziness he was experiencing. Dr. Hershewe told us in those first appointments that Kurt would need surgery to correct the anomaly, but that it could be many months, even years, perhaps before the surgery might be possible. His vision would be changing, and we would have to wait until his vision was stable before they would risk surgery. Again, we would just have to wait. But this time, it was okay.

We brought Kurt home on Valentine's Day, and it was a great day in my heart (and in his too, I know). We celebrated with balloons and blowers that didn't make any noise. Daddy was home! The girls were thrilled. We were only home a few days when we were informed that our landlord and client-friend had sold her home. It was to close escrow in thirty days or less. We would have to move.

When they heard the news, Lee and Audra phoned me with an idea. Why not come to Hawaii for the rest of the winter, get out of the cold, and Lee could help Kurt with his therapy over there? Lee was a retired PT and would work daily with Kurt, doing necessary physical and cognitive exercises. We could live in the downstairs two-bedroom apartment, and Audra would help me with the girls. How did that sound?

Like heaven on earth. Hawaii. Warm. Help. We just had to figure out how to pack up our lives again and get there.

Once again, the angel troops showed up. A crew of women friends came in to pack our entire house and move us into storage for the months we would be gone. We planned to go for the months of March and April. Amazingly, it all happened: in two short weeks we were "moved," this time into storage, and heading to Kona. Our good friend Kathy generously offered to fly over with us to help with the girls. Kurt still needed much assistance, and so did we.

Hawaii—more importantly, being with Lee and Audra—was just what the doctor ordered. We had their support and help, like real parents. They truly loved our girls and us. They needed us in some ways, with the passing of their own son, and we certainly needed them.

Lee worked intensely each day with Kurt. He not only provided Kurt with the best professional therapy physically, but he also gave of his heart, great wisdom and encouragement, as he helped Kurt mentally, emotionally, and spiritually in those difficult days. His progress seemed slow but steady. I'll never forget the day that we were all out by the pool, Kurt standing in the pool's center, when Emma (who was just two) fell in from the side. I was holding Rebecca and called to Kurt to quickly get Emmie. He seemed to get so confused that he didn't do anything. He just stood there. I knew that we were a ways from full recovery. But still, he was doing remarkably well.

It was so nice to finally be all together again, no matter where it was. We laughed at some of the silly things that he would say, unexpected silly things, and we laughed at his still funny jokes and his "Kurt" sense of humor. One morning, coming down the stairs, I heard a funny noise and silly laughter. They were all three snuggled around Dad on the bed, Rebecca tucked in the middle. He was doing his "RainBird sprinkler" imitation! Just confirmed that daddy was back.

The girls loved the time and attention given them by all of us. I realized how much we had missed any sense of normal. Lee and Audra gave me much help and a time of rest, in a way. We needed their love and support, and they were there for us. It was a special time in our lives with people that we loved. God had given us much to be thankful for.

One day, while reading my Bible, I read a passage in Exodus 17:8-16. It is the story about Moses and Aaron and Hur standing on a hillside, overlooking a battle between the Israelites and their enemies, the Amalekites. When Moses would raise his arms toward heaven, the Israelites would begin to win the battle, but when his arms grew weary, and he could not hold them up, the Amalekites would begin to win. So Aaron on one side and Hur on the other held Moses' arms up, raised toward heaven, steady until sunset.

Joshua and the Israelites won the battle that day. "Then the LORD said to Moses, 'Write this in a book as something to be remembered . . .' Moses built an altar and named it 'The LORD is My Banner' . . . ." I knew in my heart that God was confirming that I was to "write these things down as something to be remembered," to record the many miracles He had done in our lives, on our behalf. I cannot be compared to Moses, but I do know that many people had stood by my side all those months as we prayed to our God in heaven on Kurt's behalf. I knew too that the Lord truly was our banner, our great help in time of need. I wanted to heed His word to write and record His faithful working in our lives. This was one of many confirmations of the nudging to write, to record the many miracles, early on from the first days of Kurt's accident.

Scott and Sandi Tompkins were good friends of Lee and Audra's and editors of the YWAM monthly *Online* publication, as well as other books and works. The first time they came to lunch to visit with us, Sandi had words for Kurt that I knew were significant: "Kurt, expect God's best." Later, she emphasized again, "Kurt, I feel compelled to tell you to expect God's best." Sandi had heard those very words spoken to her heart when she was going into surgery to have a leg amputated below the knee. She woke up having two full legs! Those were words of life to my heart for my husband now, as they had been to Sandi then. In the midst of the steep climb back to full recovery, I believed they were for Kurt, too. Later that evening, I remember encouraging him to hang on to those words, words of hope for the journey ahead.

As the time in Hawaii was drawing to an end, we needed a place to come home to. Thankfully, we had watchmen on the wall: people were looking for a place for us to rent. Chris, Kurt's ex-business partner who was now in real estate, called to let us know that a wonderful older home just down the street from his family's home was up for rent. It would be perfect. I immediately called Jeannie; after years of friendship, we spoke each other's language, knew each other's tastes and preferences. I needed her perspective on what "perfect" meant! She gave me her report: yes, it was perfect. In fact, she called it the "Princess House"—there were lovely little rooms for the girls tucked up in the eaves of this older, delightful little house in the center of town. Again, I knew we were being taken care of.

May 1st came around, and we boarded a plane for home. I was a bit apprehensive to leave the comfort and care, and support Lee and Audra had given us, but I knew it was time for us to return to real life—normal life, whatever that meant. It was time for Lee and Audra to get back their life as well. They had graciously kept a family of five with three little ones tucked under their roof for two full months, and I knew they needed a reprieve.

This time we traveled alone. My brother picked us up late that night at the airport, as our new van had been ordered while we were in Hawaii but had not yet arrived at the dealership. It was after midnight when we arrived at our new home. As Mark helped me get the kids and suitcases into the house, I was overwhelmed by what greeted us, every room was set up perfectly, with beds made and toy animals in their right places as if waiting for the girls. Flowers on the table presided over freshly baked cookies and teacups. Pictures on the walls, food in the fridge (lots of good food!), towels hung, a note lovingly left. Everything was in its place.

Yes, indeed, this was the "Princess House," and we were again being treated like royalty. As I put each of the girls in their new beds, Kurt immediately fell into bed, exhausted. It had been a very long day for him. Although it was very late by then, I was revived by such gifts of grace. Invisible hands, precious people, had once again taken care of us. I cried tears of thankfulness. We were home.

The next morning I got up early—I was so excited to be home, *our* home, and to have peace and quiet before the troops were up. It was a beautiful, unusually warm day, so I opened the door to let in the fresh air. Mid-morning, after a late breakfast, I looked up to see Jeannie.

"I wasn't going to bother you today, but I saw your door open . . ." She hugged us all and then nudged me outside to talk.

She began to quickly tell me how she was on her way back home, heading out Highway 88 to go home with Alicia, her youngest. When they got to the intersection of Highway 88 and Mottsville, the intersection of Kurt's accident, she saw some people out in the field. She noticed that they had flowers. Initially, she didn't think anything about it. Then, suddenly, she felt the Lord saying to "go back." As she turned around, she knew in her heart that they were people somehow related to Kurt's accident. They were, in fact, the family of the two girls.

She asked me if I would like to go out to meet them if I thought Kurt would want to go. We went inside and quickly told Kurt. Yes, he wanted to go. Alicia stayed to watch Allie and Emmie; we took Rebecca with us.

As we drove out toward the intersection, Jeannie began to tell us more about her encounter. Walking into the field toward the group of five, she saw on the back of the sweatshirt of the person closest to her, *"Jesus, name above all names . . . ."* (Philippians 2:9). As the young woman turned, Jeannie said to her, "Are you the family of the kids from the accident last November?"

"Are you Shawn?" the young woman asked.

"No, but I have been involved with them from the very night of the accident! They are our dearest friends, and we have walked closely with Shawn and Kurt through this whole ordeal. Who are you all?"

"I'm Elisa, the sister of the two girls who were in the other car that night."

As she and Jeannie hugged, tears streaming down their faces, Jeannie said to her, "You're a Christian!"

"Yes," she replied. Her two parents, her husband, and a friend of the young driver were with her. "What about your parents?" No, not yet, Elisa indicated.

As they talked, the parents stepped away, and Elisa told Jeannie that both of her sisters were Christians. In fact, Mya, the oldest sister, had been in a Bible study; just a month or so before the accident, a college friend told Elisa, there had been a question in the study: "If the Lord called you home today, would you be ready?" The friend had seen Mya's response: an emphatic *Yes!*

Elisa knew where her sisters and their young friend now were: in heaven, home. Talking about her parents quietly, she told Jeannie they were not Christians, and how they sadly held onto many superstitions that were keeping them from healing, from moving forward in their grief. She said to Jeannie, "This will all be worth it if my parents come to know the Lord." She asked Jeannie to pray for them. We knew that many, many people had been—and still were—praying for them.

Rejoining her parents, who were talking with Elisa's husband and friend, they asked how Kurt was doing. Was he okay, did he recover? Was he working? Jeannie told them that he had come out of a coma and was recovering. They seemed concerned for him, for us.

The family had the pictures of the accident from the NHP, as they had received the accident report and requested the pictures. Jeannie could not believe it when she saw the pictures of the bodies lying in the field, covered with dark blue blankets. She remembered the vision the Lord had given me the night of the accident. Just like I had described.

Unfortunately, Kurt and I didn't get to see them that day. The family had already left when we arrived with Jeannie at the intersection and place of the accident.

Two months later, Elisa called me. Like my Emma, she was the middle sister of three. In talking to her, I felt like I already—somehow—knew her. She told me how her sisters and friend were driving to Mammoth that fateful night. Elisa and her husband had been married in Tahoe the weekend before, and her sisters were heading back toward home, which was in San Diego. I asked how she and her parents were doing.

She was doing fairly well, but it was time for her and her husband to move on with their lives and get their own home. They had moved in with her parents after the accident. She told me that she knew without a doubt where her sisters were: in heaven with the Lord. The young man, the driver, was a friend of theirs, having come to the U.S. from Indonesia on a student visa. Yes, he too was a Christian. Her parents, however, had not moved forward at all, still going to the gravesides nearly every day, insisting that the two girls' rooms not be changed. Life with God is tough. Life without God is nearly impossible.

My heart ached for these broken, grieving parents. How would they ever make it without God? Elisa kindly asked about us. Again, how was Kurt? How were the girls and I doing? It seemed as if we were connected by something we couldn't see. By the time the phone conversation ended, I was reminded why. Really, I was reminded, *Who*.

Recounting some of these many miracles one day with my friend, Carllene, a nurse who had helped me in many ways (especially with Kurt's many medical issues), she said to me, "It's like God is putting the pieces of this puzzle together one-by-one with His own hand, and He is signing each piece as He does it." Yes, that is exactly what it seemed like. His signature was not just on the whole puzzle, but on each and every piece.

— Chapter 4 —

His Promise

Early one morning in June, I prayed, "Please show me something. Kurt still can't see." Although Kurt was doing well overall, considering everything, he had quite a ways to go, and his vision was still very altered. I opened the Word, and God took me to John 11. It is the story of Lazarus.

Initially, Lazarus, a friend of Jesus, was sick. Jesus was told about his illness, and he delayed, saying, "This sickness will not end in death, but for the glory of God." As the story is told, Lazarus died, and Jesus came to the village and saw Lazarus' sisters, Martha and Mary, grieving with others. Jesus saw their pain, the Bible says, and *"He wept."* The shortest verse in the entire Bible, but it spoke volumes to my heart. I felt the Lord saying to me, *Kurt's pain is My pain; your suffering, My suffering.* I felt comforted by those words.

In John's text, Jesus—deeply moved by their grieving and knowing all along what He had planned to do—went to the tomb where Lazarus was buried. "Remove the stone," Jesus commanded. Not knowing what Jesus was about to do, Martha (who knew that her brother had been dead four days) basically said, "Lord, there will be a bad stench." John 11, verse 40: *"Jesus said to her, 'Did I not say to you that if you believe, you will see the glory of God?'"* Immediately, the stone was rolled away, and Lazarus came forth bound hand and foot, and his face wrapped around with a cloth. *"Unbind him, and let him go."*

I felt in my heart that God was saying He was going to heal Kurt, heal his vision. These powerful words, *"Did I not say to you that if you believe, you will see the glory of God?"* were followed by, *"Shawn, you have one job: to believe Me for the things I have shown you. To have faith."* These words were indelibly written on my heart at that moment. I believed that God would keep His word as spoken to my heart through Jeremiah 29:11. He had spared Kurt's life, and He was going to heal Kurt completely, even his vision. I would come to rely on these very words from the mouth of God for more than I could ever imagine. I had no idea what they would come to mean to me. I wrote His promise down, recorded it in my journal. This promise, these words, were forever etched in my heart and would become an anchor for my life.

That summer of '94, we began to travel to Reno, Sacramento, and San Francisco to see various neurologists, ophthalmologists, and eye surgeons. Kurt's vision was changing, not necessarily improving, so the prospect of eye surgery to correct his vision was still a ways off. We didn't know it then, but it would still be almost two years down the road before surgery would even be a reasonable consideration.

Each trip we tried to make into an adventure. Packing diapers, pull-ups, juice boxes, fruit roll-ups, blankets and pillows, the essentials, along with the girls' FAO Schwarz art boxes, their boombox, and

"Odyssey" tapes from Focus on the Family—we were ready for vacation, as the girls called it. They were great little travelers and rarely broke the family rule of "no whining." If Rebecca fussed, I'd pull over, go to the back seat of the van, nurse her and change her diaper, and we'd keep on driving. The girls loved to "Go!" Life was an adventure with them, and they were the light of our lives, making us smile and laugh. They were happy little girls who just loved life, and we loved them. We never missed a visit to the ice cream shop at Ghirardelli Square in S.F. Our favorite: a large hot fudge sundae, extra whip, no cherry, for five!

Late that summer, we decided to go ahead and begin building our new home and shop in Smith. Even though it didn't seem feasible, given Kurt's condition, his severely impaired vision, the numbness on the left side of his body, and his cognitive state at 80-85% of normal, we moved forward. The plans were submitted to the building department. Kurt and his dad drove daily out to Smith Valley to work on laying out the foundation for the shop. The excavation had been done before the accident, so we were ready to go. This would be Kurt's therapy, his way back up if it were possible. Since it was our own home, we didn't need to be pushed or stressed into meeting someone else's expectations or time-frame for building.

After returning from Hawaii, we got the accident report and now had reviewed the insurance issues. The other car had in fact run the stop sign, entering full-speed (over 50+ mph) into the highway, Kurt's car T-boning theirs. The young exchange student driver of the other car had been driving someone else's car, who had only minimal liability limits. That $30,000 was divided with the other family of the two girls who had died: they received $20,000, and we received $10,000.

At this point, it did not look like Kurt would be able to work in the near future, maybe ever, if his vision didn't improve through a miracle or medical intervention. He certainly didn't appear to ever be able to return to construction management and the work he loved. At the time, we truly didn't know if he would ever really work again.

Just before Christmas, while Kurt was still in a coma, our friend Rob mentioned that I probably needed to meet with an attorney, given the uncertainty around the accident. Rob scheduled a meeting and went with me. We discussed possible legal scenarios (in the event that the other families might sue us—a thought that *never* even occurred to me) and our own automobile insurance coverage. During that meeting with one of the partners and the young attorney, Rob's friend, it was clear that, in the end, they would take between 40-70% of what we might be awarded from a possible insurance settlement with our company. Even if they just prepared the settlement statement and it was settled without much resistance on the part of the insurance company, they would take 33% to 40% of the proceeds and then charge us for all additional costs. This would take a huge chunk of the money that was rightfully ours, money that was needed to support our young family.

Escorting us back to our car, the young attorney mentioned that he could help direct me to someone else who might aid me in preparing the settlement statement myself. Now was the time to move forward with our insurance company. We decided that summer that I would prepare the settlement statement.

I met with an attorney who specialized in tort cases, and he was kind enough to show me the basic content and required documents needed to prepare the settlement statement. I began the work of gathering the multitude of medical records, providing evidence that Kurt would most likely not be able to return to the work and profession that he knew. He had worked so hard to build the business and his reputation.

I got references from many people for whom Kurt had built custom homes or commercial buildings, testifying to his expertise in the building business and the outstanding quality of a Kurt Rowlin-built home or building. His reputation and work were essentially flawless, and these people were happy to help us now in this way. We included evidence of current and prospective jobs that now represented lost income to us. I also provided an analysis of lost future income due to Kurt not being able to return to work.

My cousin Mike, a State Farm agent and more like a brother to me, reviewed the statement and graciously helped me navigate the insurance path. That was his field of expertise; I needed his help, and he was there. Throughout that summer, we traveled to Sacramento several times, with Jeannie coming along to hold Rebecca while we met with insurance representatives and presented our case.

We prayed throughout the summer and into the fall for the outcome. We had been out of debt when Kurt had his accident. Because we had a disability policy which covered our basic expenses, we were able to make it with me staying home to take care of everyone. It took several months to get the insurance company's final declaration: we would be receiving the full amount of our underinsured/uninsured policy amount, and due to an issue known as "stacking," a loophole in the law, we would receive double our policy limits. And all this without a lawsuit to force the company to pay! Again, God had answered our prayers. He was taking care of us.

On October 1st we had the long-awaited thank you dinner that Jeannie and I had both thought of that same day while Kurt was still in ICU. We planned for almost two months. How would we get word to all the people—hundreds, literally—we wanted to invite to share in our joy of Kurt's recovery, and to thank for their gracious acts of kindness these many months? We decided to pass the invite by word of mouth and publish an invitation in the local newspaper, trusting that the right people would be there to be blessed this time by us.

Amazingly, as we were planning this dinner, a chef from Lake Tahoe who had heard of Kurt's accident and injuries contacted Jeannie and told her he wanted to volunteer himself and his staff's services for the event. They would prepare the entire meal (spaghetti, of course!); all we had to do was go shopping. We were expecting approximately three hundred people that night. We went to Costco and purchased all the food and supplies, then left the cooking to very capable hands. Again, great people with big hearts. We were so thankful and overjoyed by such a blessing.

Another good friend of ours, Shannon Johnson, volunteered to do the artwork for the "thank you" we had written for our guests. I had asked her to copy the "Footprints" poem by Margaret Fishback Powers: the poem on the card I read to Kurt the day he came out of the coma. Shannon's artwork on the front cover was perfect.

During the evening, we watched as more than three hundred people poured into the Bentley facility, which Kurt had built years ago. Jeannie and I stood with tears in our eyes, hardly believing so many would come and that we had our own personal chef cooking for us. Far better than we had imagined that night back in December. After dinner, we shared with our guests many of the stories—the miracles of God's work in our lives—over these many months. Jeannie, Robert, John, Kurt, and I each shared a little part of the story—our story—His story, really.

I shared about God's "weaving" of His will in our lives, His plans for good, Jeremiah 29:11, for Kurt, for us. Even through the darkest trials and moments, when we don't understand our circumstances, our suffering—God never leaves us or forsakes us. I ended with a poem quoted by Corrie ten Boom, called "The Tapestry":

> My life is but a weaving
> Between my Lord and me;
> I cannot choose the colors
> He weaveth steadily.
>
> Oft times He weaveth sorrow
> And I, in foolish pride,
> Forget He sees the upper,
> And I the underside.
>
> Not 'til the loom is silent
> And the shuttles cease to fly,
> Shall God unroll the canvas
> And explain the reason why.

The dark threads are as needful
In the Weaver's skillful hand,
As the threads of gold and silver
In the pattern, He has planned.

Yes, the dark threads are as necessary as the bright, beautiful golds and silvers in what He is weaving in our lives. We may not see or understand it all now, but our job is to trust Him. It was an emotional evening with tears shed, tears of joy, both by those sharing and by many of those faithful people who had walked the journey with us.

That fall, Lee and Audra, our beloved Papa and Nunie, decided to buy a home again back in our town, less than two miles from our rental home. It was so nice to have them close for most of the year. They would return to Hawaii only during the winter.

In the spring, we had the opportunity to move into the small log cabin next door to our home, which was under construction. With Kurt still unable to see well, it was an opportunity for us to live close and no longer do the daily commute each way. I could be next door, literally, and help as needed. It was a busy time and wise for us to be close so Kurt could walk to work.

I'll never forget the day during the building process when Rob and Ray came to me, so excited to tell me how they had been trying to figure out this particularly difficult roof angle on the house. They had been scratching their heads and told Kurt of their dilemma. Kurt sat down quietly on the plywood floor and began to write out some calculations. Within a few minutes, he had figured it out! The guys came to me saying, "He's back, Kurt is fully back!"

The calculations were right on, and even they, with all of their bright brains, couldn't figure it out at the moment. This, our house, was the project, the therapy that was perfectly suited for Kurt's recovery. He was doing what he loved again, although on very different terms. He was making progress. We were all thankful. I continued to hang on to the Lord's promise from John 11, believing that He was going to continue to heal Kurt completely, his vision included.

With the help of Kurt's dad, the best of friends, and carpenters and subcontractors who knew and loved Kurt, we were in our house in April '96, just about eighteen months after construction had started. Amazing!

— Chapter 5 —

The Long Climb

For the first two or more years after coming out of the coma, life was on an upward swing: Kurt was working on our house, improving in his recovery. He was not able to do things like he used to with his vision and the numbness of his left side, which limited his physical activity and work; but he didn't outwardly complain or express a great deal of frustration. In fact, I was proud of my husband, how he seemed to be coping during those first couple of years. I can say that Kurt took his new world in stride. Much was changed—everything, in a way—but we were okay, he was okay. With God's help, we would make it. Life was good: not perfect, but good.

We had met many new friends in Smith Valley and were becoming close to Jim and Tina Smith, who had four kids close in age to ours. Allie and Sarah Smith were the same age and started kindergarten together with Leslie Nuti. Leslie was the one who had prayed so fervently for Kurt from 3:00 to 4:00 am each day, believing God had made clear to her that Kurt would come out of the coma. She later gave me her "prayer" notes. How amazing that nearly two years later, Leslie was Allie's first teacher!

Like the Burns, the Smith family quickly became like family to us. Their generosity in reaching out to us began as soon as we came to the valley: they invited us into their hearts and home as newcomers to the area, and our lives would continue to be intimately entwined over the next twenty years. That old saying that "some people come into our lives for a season, others for a lifetime"—well, like the Burns family, the Smiths would be forever part of our world, our lives. We had many new friends and people in our world, as well as the faithful "old" friends.

After our home was finished, Rob and Ray decided to move to Wyoming. They doubtless had many reasons, but I think that seeing Kurt not yet able to get back into his construction business with his limitations prompted them to take the opportunity to start their own construction business out-of-state. It was hard to see them leave. Ray had been Kurt's best friend since high school, and he and Rob were the foundation of the business after Kurt's accident, completing all the projects he had started, then helping us close things down. They had done more for us than we could ever repay. It felt a little bit like some of our support was being pulled away. But we totally understood their need to start fresh in a new place, with their families, and with their own business. They were dear friends we would truly miss. I knew Kurt would greatly miss their nearly daily presence in his life.

Finally, after two and a half years, Kurt's vision was stable, confirmed by Dr. Hershewe and two eye surgeons. It had been a long wait, but it was critical to know for sure that his eyes were stable. This would be a very delicate surgery; any "overcorrection" in surgery or change in his vision could potentially make Kurt's vision *worse*. Kurt's surgery was scheduled for March 4th, 1996.

The night before we left for U.C. Davis Medical Center, friends from Smith Valley came over to our house to pray. Hardy and Marilyn Lewis, Larry and Leslie Nuti, and Bob Hargis all came and prayed for Kurt's surgery. As Hardy led in the first prayer of the night, his very first words were, "Show Yourself strong, Father."

Instantly, it came to mind that on the night of the accident, as I stood beside Kurt lying still on the gurney in the ER, Mark's repetitious cry to the Lord was, "I just love this man, Lord. Please, Father, show Yourself strong." Over and over he prayed those words in those moments in which time seemed to be standing still. At that time, I was not exactly sure what those words "show Yourself strong" meant or would ultimately come to mean to us.

Now, two and a half years later, I knew that our God had done exactly that: He had shown Himself strong. Yes, strong, all-mighty, all-knowing, all-loving, and all-merciful. Our Lord had shown Himself strong and more than faithful. He was and is still God, and He was with us in this too. I remembered Jesus' promise in John 11:40, *"Did I not tell you that if you believe, you will see the glory of God?"*

On the early morning of March 4th, at our hotel, I had some time while Kurt was getting ready to go to the hospital for the surgery. I picked up God's Word, and it opened to 2 Corinthians 1:3-4: *"Blessed be the God and Father of our Lord Jesus Christ, the Father of mercies and God of all comfort, who comforts us in all our affliction so that we will be able to comfort those who are in any affliction with the comfort with which we ourselves are comforted by God."* Certainly, both Kurt and I had the peace of the Lord in all of this.

I continued to read on, and then in verses 10b-11 of chapter 1, the Lord spoke words of life to my heart as only He can do: *He on whom we have set our hope . . . will yet deliver us, you also joining in helping us through your prayers, so that thanks may be given by many persons on our behalf for the favor bestowed on us through the prayers of many.*" Did I just read what I just read?

Immediately, my question for the Lord was, "Lord, I know that we have set our hope on You—does this mean that today, You are going to answer all of the hundreds and hundreds of prayers that have been prayed for Kurt and the restoration of his vision? Will many truly give thanks on our behalf this day for the gracious favor granted us in answer to the prayers of many?"

In my heart, I felt the answer, "Yes." Could I be positive? Was I interpreting these words correctly for our situation, for today, for Kurt? I knew this: that I felt hope and an expectancy in my heart. I pondered these verses over and over privately in my heart and mind throughout the morning.

Mark, Trina, John, and Gloria had come down that morning and met me in the waiting area. The doctor had told us it would probably take two to two and a half hours. As time continued to pass with no word, I began to get a little concerned. It had been almost three hours now. Why wasn't Kurt out of surgery yet? I didn't let my thoughts wander too far.

Finally, we received word that Kurt was out of surgery and in recovery. Shortly after, Dr. Keltner came out and talked with us. He said that he felt the surgery had gone "very well." It had been a little longer and more difficult than expected due to some things they found once they were into the surgery. But nevertheless, Kurt had done well, and both surgeons felt confident that his eyes were well aligned and that the outcome would be favorable. I remembered the words, the promises. The next morning, Kurt was scheduled for his post-op appointment with Dr. Keltner at his office. The resident physician in on Kurt's surgery, Dr. Hernandez, came in initially and took Kurt's eye measurements. They didn't seem exceptionally good or improved. Shortly afterward, Dr. Keltner came in and re-measured Kurt's excyclotorsion: the right eye measured at 1-2 degrees; the left eye was 0 degrees! He re-measured once again to be certain. Apparently, Dr. Hernandez had forgotten to adjust the eye machine correctly. Yes, those measurements were correct!

"Wow!" Dr. Keltner exclaimed. "We couldn't have gotten any closer!"

I told the doctor, "You don't know how many people were praying for Kurt and for you as the surgeon yesterday, but there were hundreds!"

He replied emphatically, "I believe it!"

Again, I called family and friends who had faithfully continued to pray for Kurt, including Mark Humphries with Focus on the Family. More than a year earlier, I had written a letter to Dr. James Dobson sharing some of our story and asking for prayer for Kurt, and specifically for his vision to be restored. Dr. Dobson's letter to us in reply assured us that they would faithfully pray for Kurt and his healing, especially his vision. I know Dr. Dobson, Mark Humphries, and dozens of others at Focus were among the "many" who had been praying all along for Kurt's vision, and all were now "giving thanks" for the gracious favor granted us.

I was—we all were—elated for Kurt. He had some weeks of healing, and about eight weeks later, he was able to get his driver's license! It had been a long time since his accident, and what an awesome privilege to be able to drive once again. It was an exciting day when we bought a "new" (used) Ford F250 for Kurt. He didn't feel like he deserved it; I knew he did. I can hardly describe the joy in seeing him drive off in his new truck heading for home.

Within a month or so, Kurt was back trying to reestablish himself and his business. Always a very hard worker, Kurt was excited to get busy again. It was an exciting time as he began another beautiful custom home in the exclusive Westwood area. He had been building a passive-solar home for Rob and Sue Anderson when I first met Kurt. Rob owned the largest civil engineering company in our area. It was Rob who had taken me to meet with the attorneys while Kurt remained in a coma.

Now, years later after a long climb back up, Kurt was building another custom French-country home for our friends along the river, facing the incredible Sierra Mountains. This was his "re-entry" back into the custom home-building industry that we weren't sure would ever happen for Kurt—for us. Needless to say, once again Kurt did an incredible job, now more as the foreman and with the help of a very good crew. And once again, many of the subs and tradespeople were there working alongside him and cheering him on.

Part Two
The Fall

— Chapter 6 —

The Shift: A Crazy World

It was during these next years that Kurt's behavior began to change, subtly at first.

He had always been a workaholic in a sense, spending much of his time at work or in his shop. His business had gotten incredibly busy during the first six years of our marriage before his accident, and I just accepted it as the only way he could keep up. Now, he spent most of his time in his shop, sometimes with not a lot going on work-wise, and he seemed to be angrier and more discontent. He was still "Kurt" in many ways, but subtly, in different ways, he seemed to be changing.

He began blaming me for things like "not letting him drink." Before the accident, he often had a beer or two at night. After the accident, the neurologist told him from the beginning it wasn't a good idea to drink, as he had lost a lot of brain cells with the injury to his brain. I had never told him not to drink, but somehow it was my fault that he couldn't. He began blaming me for being a "goody-two-shoes" Christian. I couldn't understand his insensitive attacks.

We had begun to see the pastor of the local community church for counseling. Kurt was more and more depressed, and his angry outbursts came more frequently. I was hoping that counseling would be a place where Kurt could share his frustrations, to be honest about what was bothering him.

For me, I initially just wanted to see the pastor, as I felt like I was juggling so many balls and was about to begin dropping some of them. Between Kurt and all of his issues, doctors' appointments, recovery, raising three little girls, helping my ailing mom whose health continued to decline, having moved five times in two and a half years, building a new home, and dealing with insurance issues and the myriad of daily life chores, I was getting tired.

As we talked, I began to realize that Kurt was making me feel responsible for everything in his life. Kurt had never been one to help me much at home, as he had always been busy working, which I hadn't minded so much. Now, though, he was attacking me and my character, my faith—talking about me to others, talking down to me. I had been doing most everything gladly to help him over these years, but it wasn't enough. He never asked what I might need or how I was feeling; nor did he spend much time trying to communicate or build into our marriage.

I remember telling the pastor, "I can't explain it, but he treats me like a non-person." I certainly wanted to continue to help Kurt, but I needed him to be present in our marriage and be there for me also.

He ignored my requests for help with anything, including our girls. In fact, it seemed that whatever I might ask of him, he would do just the opposite. He started wearing dirty, torn clothes each day when he had a closet full of clean things. Why would he want to look dirty and ragged-looking? Being in business, it was important to look clean, even if it is just your jeans and a chamois-cloth shirt. No matter how gently I tried to approach the subject to talk with him, he continued to dress like a homeless person. I couldn't understand why he would want to look like that. Was he doing it just to frustrate me, to make me mad or upset? Was it truly the way he felt about himself, a reflection of his own thoughts? Really, with all of our other problems, this one was nominal—but it still bothered me that he was purposely trying to look so disheveled.

One day, I had mentioned that it would be helpful if he'd offer to help do something—anything—to help me. I had started homeschooling our girls by then and was very busy with that, helping Kurt with the business now that he had returned to his construction work, and taking care of my mom. He agreed although I could tell he did so reluctantly.

I had been working in the yard trying to get it ready for a bridal shower for Karen, Jeannie's daughter. She was like a daughter to me, and the girls and I were so excited to be having her shower at our house. We wanted to have everything perfect for her and her special day.

With our yard being relatively "new," I was trying to get a lot done and had planted many new shrubs and flowers, wanting it to be beautiful for this special occasion. I worked outside in the yard at every opportunity, and it was starting to look very nice. I had planted the flower boxes on the house and around the house, and I placed two huge planter boxes at the front door entrance. I asked Kurt to water my plants. He agreed. When I went outside a little later, he had sprayed my plants so hard, with so much pressure from the hose, that the dirt from inside the planter boxes had splattered about eight feet up the stucco walls.

As I walked around the yard, he had literally stomped through my newly planted shrubs, breaking off many of the branches and flowers. I couldn't believe it. I was devastated. I had worked so hard to make everything look so beautiful, and he had intentionally destroyed my plants. Why would he do such a thing? I was so hurt and so mad and frustrated all at the same time.

When I asked him why he did it, he answered: "What, it isn't good enough for you, Shawn?" Angrily, mockingly, he said, "Nothing is ever good enough for Shawn, is it?"

Those types of words and explanations for his behavior became more and more frequent. Somehow, I was to blame for his actions. He certainly knew how to make sure I didn't ask him for any help. But I sensed the issues were deeper than the request, deeper than the feeling of being "put out" when I asked him to help. It was his way of getting back at me. But why was he beginning to act like this more and more? Over time, I saw this type of passive-aggressive behavior more apparent with Kurt. I didn't know why he was acting like he did, but I could see the patterns. Needless to say, I rarely asked him to do anything.

He was angry about the accident, angry about his condition, angry at me. He blamed himself, he said, for killing those other three kids. Even though the other driver had clearly caused the accident by running the stop sign, Kurt began this type of self-flagellation, self-condemnation. He believed in God, he said, but he could not be saved. I talked with him, sharing that Christ died for all of us—did he believe that? Yes, he did, but he still thought he couldn't be saved.

He talked about being a scumbag, a "nothing." I couldn't understand what was happening with my husband. He began to talk about not being saved, not being right with God. I wanted so to see him have some peace and believed that God could help him. He seemed to have self-hatred and loathing that I had never seen in him before. I felt sad and sorry for him and tried to comfort and help and encourage him. He hid out more and more in his shop. Most days he would only come in for dinner, and then it was off early to bed, usually with an argument. Often, I could smell alcohol, but he would deny that he'd been drinking.

If I would try to talk to him about drinking, he would only get angry. What did I care? "I'm not drinking. You're just paranoid because your dad drank! I bet you wish I had been killed in that accident, don't you?" he would blurt out angrily. I couldn't reason with or convince him that he was loved by me, the girls, the Lord. He just kept saying he should have died in the accident.

One late afternoon, Kurt stormed out of the house, angry about something. I saw him grab a gun out of the closet, so I followed him. I literally jumped on his back, trying to keep him from going up the mountainside behind our home as he carried his rifle, not wanting to return. After I wrestled him off the mountainside and coaxed him back home, he told me he was sorry for his actions, saying he didn't know what was wrong with him. That night, I took all of his guns over to my brother's.

His angry words, irrationality, self-deprecating attacks, lowly self-image, and increasingly destructive behavior made it seem that something other than depression was driving his mind, his actions. I prayed and prayed for my husband, often getting up with him early in the morning and then staying on the couch pouring my heart out to God, before our three little girls would climb out of bed and we would begin our day together. I remembered God's promise from John 11 the summer after Kurt's accident, *"Did I not tell you if you believe, you will see the glory of God?"* I began to pray for Kurt's mental, emotional, and spiritual healing.

Sadly, Kurt was rarely around, and it seemed like he was slipping farther and farther away from us. His behavior was getting stranger, more unpredictable, and our relationship more and more strained. We didn't have any real intimacy: no talking or real communication, often just arguing about sex. He would approach me more often and at inappropriate hours. He seemed to have no regard for me. When he didn't get his needs met, he would call me names.

At the time I found it hard to attribute these troubling changes to the head injury, telling myself that more than two years had gone by after the injury with none of these symptoms. So it didn't seem like that could be the cause—at least, not fully the cause. It has only been very recently that I began to learn more about how profoundly brain injuries can affect personality and behavior, and how sometimes symptoms can take a long time to appear. But at the time, I didn't know that. It was hard not to blame Kurt, to feel that he was deliberately choosing to treat me this badly.

His erratic behavior seemed to be completely unexplainable at times—confusing, to say the least. One weekend afternoon, I went into Kurt's shop to check on him and also to help clean it out and help him organize his tools, plans, and paperwork. Kurt repeatedly mentioned how overwhelmed he was. I offered to come out to the shop to help.

Walking into the shop, Kurt looked up. "What are you doing in here?" he asked, seeming agitated.

"I just came out to help you, to help you get things organized like we had talked." I went by his drafting table and began to organize some papers, sweeping off the sawdust. Starting to talk to him, I moved a few things around, and as I bent over, opening a trunk underneath the table, his voice grew angry. "Get out of here!"

"What . . . ? I just came out to . . ." I started to reply, confused.

"I don't want *your* help! I don't need *your* help! *Get out of here!*" Coming around the table abruptly, *"Get out!"* he growled, literally chasing me out of the shop.

I ran toward the house, confused and almost scared of his reaction to me. I couldn't believe it.

I went into the house to gather my thoughts, trying to figure out what was wrong with Kurt. Why did he react like that, treat me like that? He charged and chased me almost in an animal-like, growling way. I really couldn't believe it. For the first time, I packed up our young girls in the van and drove to town.

Life was getting crazier and crazier, it seemed. There were times he would leave and not come home. One afternoon, he left angry, speeding so fast down our gravel driveway that I could see the back end of his truck sliding sideways; I thought the bed of his truck might hit the fence gate. I watched as he raced up the driveway to our neighbors' house. I didn't think they were home, as it was in the middle of the day. He was there for just a few minutes and then sped off. He didn't return that night.

Of course, I couldn't sleep and wondered whether I should call the sheriff's office to report him missing. I prayed through most of the night. Finally, at about 10:00 a.m. the next day, he came home. His clothes and face and hands were filthy as if he had rolled in the dust and then in the mud.

He told me how he had gone to the neighbors' and had taken one of their guns out of the closet. He then drove to the local mercantile, bought a 12-pack of beer, and headed up into the Sweetwater Mountains. He had raced his truck so madly up the mountain that he had a flat tire and had to stop. In his rage, he hiked up to a big tree, opened up the first can of beer, and guzzled it down. After guzzling the second beer, he put the muzzle of the rifle in his mouth. He was going to end it all. He described how the ants were crawling on him, biting him. He opened a third can of beer.

Then he said he realized what he was doing, to leave us like that—and he suddenly couldn't pull the trigger. I tried not to cry. I was so relieved, but I was mad at him, too. Why hadn't he come home yesterday? He said he knew I'd be mad.

"Of course I'd be upset," I said, "but you still should have come home. Where did you stay all night?"

"On the mountain," he said. I told him he couldn't keep doing these things. I told him that we loved him and needed him. He said he was sorry. He asked, "What is wrong with me?"

I didn't know. It just seemed like he was incredibly angry with me, himself, perhaps God. Only God knew for sure. Kurt couldn't seem to figure out what was wrong. I certainly couldn't.

— Chapter 7 —

Cries of a Desperate Heart

It is difficult to describe the heart cries of a woman who sees her man slipping away mentally and emotionally, a man whose behavior has changed, especially toward you as his wife. I was devastated. I didn't know what to do to help Kurt.

Before the pastor in Smith Valley was to leave on an extended vacation, he realized the desperate place Kurt was in. He was in obvious turmoil, admitting to the pastor his rage, and even sharing his desire at times to "end it all." That's when the pastor referred us to Christian psychologists in Reno.

From our first visit, it seemed that this couple had some professional insight into Kurt's actions and accusations. By the end of our second session, the husband of the team started seeing Kurt one-on-one. I would be asked to come into the appointments from time to time. Kurt had been on anti-depressants on and off, as he chose to take them—Jim would help him with that issue as well. Right away, he performed a personality and mental health assessment on Kurt.

The next week when Kurt came home with the results of the tests, he handed me the paperwork and said, "You are married to one screwed up guy." I remember saying to him that we are all messed up, all have issues that we need to work on. He didn't stay to read through the results with me, but later that evening, when I had time to look at the analysis, I learned that Kurt had several "personality" disorders, primarily passive-aggressive and schizoid.

The passive-aggressive issue did not surprise me; but initially, when I read the word "schizoid," I immediately thought "schizophrenia" and thought, "Oh, no, he can't have schizophrenia! No wonder we are having problems!" But as my eyes settled on the word in front of me, *schizoid*, I read the short description following: "Persons with this disorder often have trouble in social situations, in maintaining personal and work relations, often work alone . . ." I looked up a more thorough definition of this condition in the Mayo Clinic Health book and found the following: *SPD, schizoid personality disorder, is often characterized by a lack of interest in social relationships, a tendency towards a solitary lifestyle, secretiveness, emotional coldness, and apathy. Affected individuals may simultaneously demonstrate a rich, elaborate, and exclusively internal fantasy world.* I didn't think Kurt was dealing with an internal fantasy world, but the other symptoms—lack of interest in social relationships, solitary lifestyle, apathy—yes, those were apparent.

After reading the detailed description of schizoid behavior disorder, the very last line jumped out at me (right off the page, or so it seemed): *"There is no known cure. . . ."*

I sat back, startled, staring at the words. *No known cure.* Well, no known cure, perhaps, to man, I thought. But nothing is "unknown" or hidden from God, and with Him *all things* are possible. I was not going to take this word as absolute truth or a final diagnosis. God would provide help to Kurt through counseling, help in learning to cope in constructive ways. I again prayed and asked God to please help us, give us direction for Kurt, bring hope and health and healing to Kurt, to us, to our marriage, and to our family. *Help me, Lord, to trust You.* I believed that God would see us through these issues.

The next week, I went in to see the psychologist to talk about the results of Kurt's testing. After he explained these personality traits or disorders to me again, I asked him if these were perhaps caused by, or were a result of, his head injury. No, he stated emphatically. These problems developed way back.

"Way back? What do you mean by that?"

"Probably from his earliest childhood years," he stated.

I somehow felt a sadness for Kurt, not knowing what, in his distant past, could have caused him to have to learn to cope in such unhealthy ways. I knew his mom was extremely controlling and at times exposed her own manipulative behavior patterns for all to see, pouting to get attention, not talking, walking out of conversations, stomping off to her bedroom, slamming doors when not getting her way. His dad in all of this was always very passive. Now I realized that Kurt's strange ways of coping were developed back from his early boyhood. I only felt more compassion for him and wanted to see him get help.

From this point on, the doctor insisted Kurt come in for counseling two to three times per week. He said it would be best if it was every day, but that was impossible. This new information just caused me to pray for my husband more and more. For God's help. For God's healing.

Looking back now at this assessment from the psychologist—that Kurt's coping skills were developed in his childhood—I can see on the one hand how this was helpful information. But on the other hand, it would have been so much more helpful at the time for the counselor to address not only Kurt's developed ways of coping, but also the fact that his head injury *was* a significant factor adding to his confusion and his way of presently dealing with—or not dealing with—issues. His traumatic brain injury could explain his dramatic behavioral shift in some ways.

What might have been different, I wonder, if Kurt had been able to think about himself not as "one screwed up guy" but as someone showing behaviors that—while scary—are typical symptoms for people with extreme brain injury? He might have been able to recognize that he was normal, not exceptionally messed up—that he was not alone—that he needed and could find help. Instead, it seems he dove fully into the shame-driven belief that he was fundamentally flawed, incapable of producing anything but pain and harm for himself and those he cared most about. And those beliefs . . . well, so often they become self-fulfilling prophecies.

It was during these years that Kurt had begun to pursue me almost relentlessly about sex. Somehow it seemed all-important, all-encompassing to him. It didn't matter what time of night it might be, or how I might be feeling, or the circumstances; he just seemed to need and want more sex. I couldn't figure out what was going on with him, but I kept thinking that it was his need for love and affirmation. He had lost much of his ability to do the same kind of physical work he used to do, and I thought perhaps this was his way of feeling better about himself as a man. But often, his approaches came at inappropriate times when it was so late, when I was exhausted and had no energy. It seemed like he had no sense of my world or how I felt—it was just about what he needed, getting his needs met with no regard for me. If I didn't respond to his advances, he would call me names and even follow me into another room and try to get into the twin bed with me.

Our relationship was more and more strained. We argued and fought. No real intimacy. No real relationship. So to have him relentlessly pursuing me was hurtful. He began calling me names, telling me I was frigid, telling me I was cold-hearted, and talking to others, including my own brothers, about our sex life. I was embarrassed and felt "uncovered," to say the least. All along, he was talking to his parents, who felt sorry for him. I became like the "other woman." They would hang up on me if I answered the phone when they called. Later, they called him only directly on his shop line or cell phone and even stopped sending our girls cards on their birthdays. I couldn't figure it all out and didn't have the energy to try.

When I would try to talk to Kurt about how he was treating me, he would respond that my body was not my own: the *one* scripture he seemed to remember. I would try to talk rationally with him, telling him that he shouldn't be treating me the way he was, calling me names, being so inconsiderate, waking me up at all hours of the night, talking terribly about me to others. I was his wife, and he should be my covering, my protector: not someone who is intentionally trying to hurt me.

How would any woman respond to such disrespect? No wife would want to have a physical or sexual relationship with him acting this way. To him, I was simply one thing: frigid. It wasn't his fault; it was mine. What was wrong with me?

Well, for one, I was getting worn out. Kurt's behavior and the stress of everything were starting to take their toll on me after four-plus years. I had been diagnosed with chronic fatigue and mononucleosis, and there was no way for me to just rest. With three little girls, now homeschooling, managing the administrative and financial side of our business, and in some ways taking care of Kurt, along with taking care of my mom, I was exhausted. But I couldn't just stop. I kept going, getting help with diet and supplements, and sleeping when I could. But even being that sick and worn out didn't stop Kurt's advances.

One of my few close friends in whom I had confided, Lori, began to ask, "Do you think Kurt could have a problem with pornography or something?"

"I don't think so. He never looks at other women like that. I've never seen any evidence, magazines or anything else. I think it's probably because his world has changed so much. Losing some of his physical abilities, not being able to do all the things he used to do. Somehow, I think it relates to his manhood, to his feeling inadequate, perhaps." I was certain in my heart that pornography wasn't an issue for Kurt.

It seemed the more we disagreed and argued about sex, the worse Kurt's behavior got. After taking the guns to my brother's, Mark came up to our house, wanting to know what was happening and why I had brought the guns to their house. He also asked why we "couldn't just get along." *Long story*, I thought.

Trying to help, he asked what each of us wanted to see changed most in our marriage. I responded to his question saying that I would like to see us be able to deal with our issues in a rational, honest way, seeing resolution and change. When he asked Kurt the same question, Kurt said he would like to have more sex. I could see the surprise on Mark's face. He then asked Kurt exactly what he was talking about. Every day, if possible: four, five, or six times a week. Again, I felt "exposed," which was becoming more and more common, with Kurt talking to nearly anyone who would listen about me, our sex life—or the lack of it, according to him.

It was during this time of absolute confusion that the Lord became known to me as *The One Who Knows All Things*. What was causing my husband to act like someone I didn't know? Was it his head injury? Was it something else? I knew that Kurt was struggling with depression and some guilt, perhaps, but somehow his strange behavior didn't seem to me that it was all (or mostly, even) "head injury" related. His first couple of years post-head injury were easy compared to the years now as we seemingly tried to trudge ahead when truly we were sinking deeper and deeper. He hadn't acted like this in those first two or three years.

Now more and more he was acting like a child—not so much child-like, but self-centered, self-absorbed, almost narcissistic. Everything was about him and his needs, his desires. He didn't have a clue about me or the girls, really. Though I had spent years helping him through his recovery, he didn't even seem to be able to ask how my own doctor's appointments went—did I have chronic fatigue, mono? How was I feeling? He either didn't seem to care or was too overwhelmed to think to ask. He didn't offer much help with the girls. I knew he loved them, but even with them, he didn't seem to connect or want to connect. Slipping farther and farther away from us, I didn't know what to do to reel him in.

I spent a lot of time early in the mornings, in the Word, praying and asking God to show me what was going on with Kurt. Was it his head injury? Was it . . . something else, just his inability to face things?

God had given me that promise, the summer of 1994, *"Did I not tell you if you believe, you will see the glory of God?"* I remember praying many times, *"Lord, I don't know what is wrong with Kurt, but You do. All those years ago, You gave me that word, that promise in John 11. Back then I believed You for Kurt's physical healing, and You have healed him, for the most part, physically. But You, being the One who knows all things, knew that we would be going through this years later. I want to believe You now for his healing mentally, emotionally, and even spiritually. I want to see Your glory, Lord. I want to see Your glory. Please heal Kurt's heart and mind and soul. Heal our marriage. Help us."* My heart's cry over and over, out of absolute desperation.

Our world was truly falling apart, but still, I had one job: to believe Him, to believe the Lord for the promises, for His words to me. I wanted to believe. God had done so much for us, sparing Kurt's life, healing him physically—those "many miracles beyond measure" that He had so graciously performed, done on our behalf—how could our lives have fallen so far? We certainly weren't honoring Him with our lives now, I thought. Surely with all our problems, fighting, arguing, angry confrontations daily, sinning . . . we weren't bringing Him glory. I felt like we had let God down.

But God pours out His love on us whether we are in sin or out of it, broken or whole, walking upright or lost. The One who knows all things, sees all things. I knew He saw my broken heart.

I couldn't believe our marriage was falling apart, that Kurt's life was so out of control, causing mine and the girls' to be severely affected. He seemed to want to take himself down with his self-destructive behavior and attitudes. At times, all I could do was cling to God. Life was so confusing.

— Chapter 8 —

Under the Covers

Life continued to march forward, even though we seemed more than a bit crippled by the problems in our lives. I was busy with the girls, home-schooling them, and they were getting busy with dance and other outside activities. Since we lived a bit further out, I had encouraged the girls to choose one sport, one "activity," that they each loved. When they all landed on the dance floor over the years between the ages of five and eight, it was clear: they each had found their passion. We began to spend much time in town, hours and hours at the dance studio.

It was such a joy to watch our girls—each one individually, and as sisters—share such a passion, such a pursuit. And they did it whole-heartedly. It was amazing to watch them begin to explore every area of dance, from ballet to jazz and tap, lyrical, and hip-hop. It seemed they were all three made for this one thing, and they gave it their all, each year growing in their talent and love for this art. Kurt and I were both proud of them in so many ways. Even in the hard times of a marriage, the hardest of times, our kids still tie us together. I know ours did.

On a rare weekend, we went away to Sacramento to attend Kurt's parents' fortieth wedding anniversary. We had gone down the afternoon before the party and checked into our hotel (one with a swimming pool, of course) to relax and have some family time. The minute we got to the room, the girls' pleas to go to the pool started in unison. It had been a long drive, and it would be good for all of us to get into the water, swim, exercise a bit, and have some fun. I got the girls ready and got our bags together. Kurt decided that he would stay back in the room to rest as he was tired from the drive.

When I got to the pool, I realized that I had forgotten our towels. Not wanting to drag all the girls back to the room, I stayed for a little while and then, meeting another mom with several kids our girls' ages, I asked if she would mind watching Allie, Emma, and Becky for a few minutes. I ran to the room and headed in to get the towels in the bathroom. Kurt had been watching TV and shut it off, saying he was tired and going to sleep. I quickly left, towels in hand, to return to the pool and our girls. We would be back in an hour or so.

We went to the anniversary dinner and headed back for home the next day. About two weeks later, I received the VISA statement with the charge for our hotel room. I knew what the room charge had been, but for some reason, it was incorrect on the statement. I called the hotel and asked for someone to help me review and correct the charges.

As I talked to the gentleman on the phone, yes, the room charges were what I thought they were. That was fine. There was an extra charge on the bill, though, for a movie rental.

"Oh, we didn't rent a movie; in fact, we've never rented a movie in a hotel room and wouldn't even know how to do that," I insisted.

"Was your room number 459?" he asked me.

Yes, it was. The man put me on hold and then came back on the line. "This charge is for an adult movie."

"Oh, no, that can't be right, we're Christians and have three little girls—we would never watch that kind of movie! This has to have been charged to the wrong room somehow." My words were sincere and convincing. The young man put me on hold, and he came back saying that the hotel would reverse the charges.

Only after I hung up did I remember that Kurt had been watching TV.

It was more than a year later that Kurt and I went to a Christian seminar aimed at helping people to face the difficult issues in their lives. My friend Marsha had recommended it and suggested that we both attend one of these Christian retreat weekends. I did not want to go with Kurt, thinking that perhaps we would both be freer to face our own issues alone rather than battling through a weekend together. Kurt was the first to attend one of these seminars in Nashville.

About a week after he returned home, he told me that he had some things to share with me. Specifically, one of the "truths faced" in this rather confrontational seminar/workshop was the destructive power of lies in a marriage. Kurt said that he had not been honest about a couple of things: first, that he had been drinking in his shop (which I knew, of course), and second, that he had attended a men's club once.

He went on to give me some of the details which I didn't necessarily want to know, but he said that he was sorry. He continued to offer me an explanation of just how he "ended up at this place" in downtown Reno after an eye doctor appointment and how his friend

Nick had wanted to go there. His "explanation" didn't seem to add up; there was more than a bit of contradiction as he explained why they just "had to stop" at this men's club. Also, I didn't think that Nick would be someone to go to that type of club. He got frustrated with me asking questions. The conversation ended abruptly, with him once again telling me that I just didn't trust him and always had to wear the pants in the family. My problem. Yes, my problem. Our problem, really.

The next morning, Kurt approached me very early before dawn. When I told him that his dishonesty had been hurtful, that we needed to talk about some things, he immediately got mad, got up, showered, and headed outside to his shop.

Mid-morning, the phone rang. It was a woman from Kurt's small group at the weekend workshop he'd just attended. She was calling to check in with Kurt, to see how he was doing. I went out to the shop to let Kurt know that she was on the phone. I couldn't find him in the workshop. I called loudly for him; even if he was back behind the shop or house, he could have heard me calling for him. I returned to the phone to let the woman know I hadn't found him but that he was here and would call her back shortly, or if she preferred, she could give him a call in fifteen minutes or so. She was happy to call back.

I headed back to the shop to try to find Kurt. I called and called and went around the back side of the property. I even whistled, wondering if he had headed up the mountain. Surely he could hear me. I had a few moments of thoughts I didn't want to think and finally decided to check the last place I could think of: the chicken coop.

As I entered through the inner door of the coop, I saw Kurt, lying on his side in the middle of the filthy floor, his face toward the door, chickens hopping all over him.

"What are you doing?" were the only words that would come out of my mouth.

"This is where I belong," he stated flatly.

"Well, I don't know if this is where you belong, but you just received a phone call . . . she'll be calling back in a little while." Shocked to see my husband lying in a coop, laden with chicken poop and with chickens scrambling over his body, I really didn't know what else to say.

Kurt told me to take the call for him.

"No, she wants to know how you are doing, Kurt. You can talk to her directly—you tell her how you are doing."

I left the coop frustrated, angry and confused by Kurt's behavior. He seemed like a little kid throwing a fit. He didn't get his way that morning, so this must be his way of "pouting" or torturing himself, or me. Really, I didn't have much sympathy for him.

Surprisingly, Kurt came into the house and went directly into the office. Not too long after, the phone rang. It was his woman friend from the conference. I listened from the corner of the sunken living room: *He was doing fine. The conference had been a great help to him.* Really??? That was quite far from the truth. It seemed like he was not being truthful, even with others.

At the time, Kurt's behavior was completely baffling. Seeing him face down in a filthy chicken coop feeling like he belonged there was more than perplexing. But looking back, with a lens of an understanding of shame and how shame works, it all makes a lot more sense.

Dr. Brené Brown, a research professor at the University of Houston, has done extensive work in studying shame and its effect on people, their view of themselves, and how it affects not just their thoughts but their actions. We are all made for love and connection; God made us for relationship with Him and with others. In Brown's words, we are all "hardwired" for love and belonging.

Shame devastates a person's sense of self-worth. Shame says to its victim, "You are not worthy; you are not lovable; you don't belong." With shame, the focus is on self: "I *am* bad. I *am* a mistake." We tell ourselves we're idiots, losers, no good. Shame tells us that there is something profoundly, deeply wrong with us. According to Brown, "it is the intensely painful feeling that we are flawed—and therefore, we are unworthy of love and belonging."

Shame is different from guilt. With guilt, the focus is not on self but on behavior: "I *made* a mistake," not "I *am* a mistake." Guilt's self-talk is, "I *did* something bad." Unlike shame, which exacerbates the problem, guilt can spur us on to better, changed behavior, because guilt encourages us to see when our behavior doesn't line up with our deepest values. When we believe that we're *not* just bad and worthless but rather are *doing* something we don't like in ourselves, we can then believe that we are, in fact, capable of change. Shame, however, keeps us in a swampland of despair: sensing our utter unworthiness. It pulls us deeper into the cesspool which threatens to destroy our sense of being loved and loveable—our sense of belonging and connection.

Now I can see Kurt's struggle more clearly. Shame was telling him—as it came out in his very own words to me many, many times—"I'm a scumbag. I'm nothing." Shame was calling him to wallow in a poop-laden chicken coop. In his mind, that's where he belonged. He had no other story to tell about himself but that he was, at his core, a "screwed-up guy" who belonged there. Sadly, the enemy—shame—had caused him to believe the lie.

Life, our lives, continued to limp along. Kurt was fortunate to be selected as the general contractor on a major remodel of a 16,000 square foot beautiful Tahoe home with magnificent views of the lake. The owners had purchased a golf course in the Carson Valley, and Kurt had come highly recommended as one of the few contractors capable of such a challenging, high-end project.

This was an extensive job: fully remodeling a gourmet kitchen, upgrading bathrooms throughout the home, rebuilding decks, refurbishing bedrooms and "bunk rooms" for all of the grandkids, adding a phenomenal entertainment "suite," and more. Nothing was missed, and the materials selected by the owners were chosen from Italy, France, and other places around the world. Their tastes were exquisite; only the highest quality materials and craftsmanship would suffice. I knew that Kurt was rightly chosen; he still loved his work, his craft, and worked hard to please his clients. He would do a great job. With me managing the business end of things, we still made a good team in some ways.

Toward the end of the job, the couple was clearly thrilled with their "new home" and appreciative of all Kurt had done to make it all they wanted. They extended an invitation to Kurt and me to fly up to Alaska and meet them and their crew for a twelve-day excursion on their exclusive yacht, the Lady Diane, named after Mario's favorite girl: his wife. They extended the invitation to include our girls as well if we wanted to bring them along. But they wanted us to decide; either way was fine with them. We had never really been anywhere without them for an extended period of time, and what an adventure it would be for them as well. Seemed like it couldn't be real, that we would have such an opportunity. We were graciously being offered a dream vacation by our clients, now friends. We couldn't believe it!

We flew up to Juneau where we were met at the airport and shuttled to the dock to board the 100-foot beauty. When Mario and his crew met us, they extended the umbrellas over our heads, all five of us, to keep us dry, and escorted us to a place that one might only dream of. I thought as they greeted us with such care, "Don't they know who we are? We aren't 'somebodies'—we are just a common, average family, really." Yet they treated us like we were "somebodies." It felt like I was in a bit of a Cinderella dream, being shuttled by a fanciful carriage to an incredible ball.

Our days were filled with food: delicious foods of every kind, specially prepared meals by a world-class chef, wines paired with different courses if we wanted to indulge—lovely menus awaiting us at our table each meal. It is hard to describe the joy of sitting at a table expectant of a fabulous, truly gourmet meal prepared just for you. Oh, how special we all felt.

At first, the chef prepared separate meals like pasta or burgers for the girls. At that stage, they were still not big eaters but liked most food. I felt bad that

Michelle, the chef, was having to make two separate meals—one for the children, one for the adults—for both lunch and dinner. I mentioned to Mario and Diane that she didn't have to do that for our kids. They could basically share our food. They were shocked and delighted. Their own grandkids were rather picky and liked more typical "kid" foods so they couldn't believe that our girls would eat all kinds of fish, seafood, spicy sauces, and delicious desserts (of course!).

We so enjoyed our time with our friends and their great staff. We learned how Mario had been recruited by a head-hunter to take a huge savings and loan out of receivership with the goal of turning it around. Not only did he do that, but he also did it within a few short years, and the remuneration promised him for success came in a few years, blessing them financially beyond what they could have ever dreamed. Here they were now blessing ordinary people like us with a trip, an adventure of a lifetime. We were treated like royalty in every way.

During the day, we would watch the orcas dive and play next to the yacht, soak in the spa at the back of the boat while drinking in the phenomenal views of the Alaskan coastline and waters. We watched the glaciers calve, the eagles soar, and pretended that this was our life! We rode Seadoos and hiked on the islands, watching the huge brown bears feed on salmon running up the streams. It was, in many ways, like a dream, like a fairytale. We played games with the girls, they "tubbed" in the big bathtub filled to overflowing with bubbles, and they even took cooking classes with chef Michelle. Each day, we truly were being lavished with goodness and graciousness from our special friends.

At night, though, I dreaded going to our room. I knew that Kurt and I would have arguments over one thing. How sad that such a damper could be put on this whole amazing experience. When he would not leave me alone, I would retreat into the tiny private bathroom, hoping no one would hear our muted arguing. Oh, sometimes I wanted to strangle him—he just seemed to be like a robot, chasing me like an animal. I wanted to scream but didn't. The Cinderella ball would end with the day; I felt like the soot-covered, rag-clad Cinderella at night. I was exhausted by the arguing and fighting over this.

— Chapter 9 —

Ashes: A Charred and Barren Land

My mom's health continued to decline over the years. The girls and I would go to see her a couple of times a week at the convalescent home where she lived. She was no longer walking, and at times she would just be slumped down in her wheelchair, not able to talk or communicate much with us. While the medication made her erratic movements decrease and controlled her anxiety, it also seemed that the dosages were at times too much, causing her to be less responsive. It was hard to see her so compromised. The doctors really didn't seem to know what to do for her, so they would occasionally change her medications to appease my brother's and my appeals for more effective help for her. It was difficult to watch her decline.

Life had been hard on my mom. When I was fifteen, my parents divorced, and over the next decade, my mom seemed to slip downward emotionally and physically. She had once been very capable, intelligent, and beautiful. For a long time, she became angry, bitter, and resentful, especially toward my dad. And though we had been through some bitter years together, she seemed to change after Kurt's accident. She was less self-centered, more concerned about Kurt and about us. Over these past few years, I knew that she had come to trust in the Lord. Though she couldn't communicate well, I knew her heart had been changed.

It was a cold day in mid-December. I had gone to town with the girls to get my hair cut. While at the salon, the nursing home called to say that my mom wasn't doing well. I had thought that we would go by to see her, but I wasn't feeling great and mentioned that I didn't want to give her my germs. The nurse on the other end of the line then told me that my mom was really not well; she was not able to transfer, had been in bed all day, and her limbs were turning purple. Did that mean her circulation was extremely poor? I asked. She didn't answer; I just needed to come. I called Jeannie, and she came and got the girls for me.

As I entered my mom's room, I knew immediately that this was it: her green eyes were like little slits barely open for me to see them. I felt a sudden grief and sadness as I sat by her, holding her hand. Tears streamed down my face; I couldn't keep them back, even in front of her. It had been a long journey, but she was still—and would always be—my mom. I loved her and now appreciated her more as a mom than I had before. She had not done everything right, but who of us has? I know I have done things wrong with my own kids, that I haven't been a perfect mom either, even though I want to be with all my heart. My mother had a very hard life in some ways, and not always as a result of her own choices. My heart hurt for her years of pain.

In a faint whisper, she said, "Don't cry. I want to go." I knew what she meant, and I wanted that for her, too: to be finally at peace, to rest, no longer struggling with the cares and pain of this world. Heaven is so grand, so great, that I think that God limits what He tells us about it in the Bible because we would have a difficult time truly perceiving it, truly grasping how wonderful it will be for those of us who believe. I wanted her to be in paradise, but it was hard to let go.

I called my brothers and sister and stayed with her that night, leaving at about 11:00. When I finally crawled into bed about midnight, Kurt began to pursue me. He didn't seem to have any sense of my world. "Kurt, I am exhausted," I said to him. "My mom is dying, and I don't have anything to give. Nothing."

"Then get the ____ out of here!" He put his foot on the small of my back and pushed me out of bed. I did get the heck out of there and went up into one of the girl's rooms. I was so exhausted, I didn't even care about Kurt or our issues at the moment. It really didn't matter.

That weekend, my mom passed away. All three of my siblings were there at some point. My younger sister, Chris, stayed the week with me. We were all grieving with the passing of our mom. I was also feeling sad about my dying marriage. It was December. In my heart, too, it felt like December—but like Christmas would never come again.

The next summer, I had taken the girls and gone into Carson City to spend a day and night at our rental, getting it cleaned up for the next renters (making some minor repairs and painting). It was also a break from Kurt and our fighting. As we were returning home, about ten miles or so from Smith Valley we noticed that it seemed smoky.

As we turned on Lower Colony Road, I could tell there was a fire on the mountains north of us. With the last turn, we could see that the fire was directly behind our home. Alternatingly, an airplane was dropping a red fire retardant, while a helicopter was dropping huge buckets of water. There were dozens of trucks and an army of firefighters all around. As we got closer, a sheriff stopped us, saying that we couldn't proceed any further due to the fire. "That's our house!" I exclaimed. He cautiously let us through, but only to go down to the ranch below. I took the girls down to our neighbors until I knew more about the situation.

It was apparent that the fire had started some time earlier that day, and the fire crews were making good progress in getting it contained. Our house was still standing, but we could see the flames. Fire was engulfing trees higher up the mountain while smoldering trees and shrubs were right behind our home.

Chris, our good friend, and neighbor, met me on the driveway. I asked him what had happened, and he said they thought a spark from a fence repairman's torch had started the fire. I then asked if he knew where Kurt was. Chris had called him about three hours ago to tell him about the fire; Kurt had been working on a remodel in Tahoe. Chris didn't know why he hadn't returned yet.

As I got to the house, it was amazing to watch dozens of firefighters on the mountain, the Bureau of Land Management property right beyond our backyard, working to contain the fire. It was still burning higher up the mountain but was now only smoldering directly behind our house. Even the fence and trees in our backyard were burned. It was difficult to breathe with the ash and smoke caused by the ravaging fire. It had come within ten feet of two 500-gallon propane tanks. If it hadn't been for our neighbor Marv—a retired fireman from L.A.—seeing the flames and coming to the aid of those two young fence repairmen, the entire mountain could have blown up.

Tina called and offered to pick up the girls and take them home for the night. As I thanked her, Kurt drove up in his truck. I asked why he hadn't come home sooner? A client's wife was having surgery that afternoon, and Kurt had said that he would come by the hospital in Tahoe. Even though she wasn't going to be awake or responsive, Kurt chose to visit her instead of coming home, even when he knew about the fire.

A short while later, I saw that Kurt had gone to get his five-gallon bucket and was feeding the birds around the house! We had probably 75-80 or more people around with a smoldering mountain right at our back door, and he was feeding the birds. I couldn't believe it. After he fed the birds, he went into his office to pay bills. It seemed he just had to "check out."

Looking back now at Kurt's actions, I realize that there was more going on with him than just "bizarre" behavior. I knew then that his brain injury was a factor, but I didn't fully comprehend the physiological changes that can occur following trauma. Even years after his traumatic brain injury, there could be significant changes in the brain driving his baffling behavior: not showing up when our home was nearly in flames and the mountain on fire, feeding the birds, doing office work during an emergency. Many factors were affecting his behavior—his brain injury perhaps not the least of these.

Dr. Bessel van der Kolk, M.D., is the founder and medical director of the Trauma Center in Brookline, MA. He is also a professor of psychiatry at Boston University School of Medicine and director of the National Complex Trauma Treatment Network. In his book *The Body Keeps the Score: Brain, Mind, and Body in the Healing of Trauma*, van der Kolk explains that trauma (whether caused by direct, physical injury to the brain, or by mental, emotional, physical or sexual abuse) alters the brain and body's functioning in ways that may produce aberrant behavior:

> Research . . . has revealed that trauma produces actual physiological changes, including a recalibration of the brain's alarm system, an increase in stress hormone activity, and alterations in the system that filters relevant information from irrelevant . . . . These changes explain why traumatized individuals become hypervigilant to threat at the expense of spontaneously engaging in their day-to-day lives. They also help us understand why traumatized people so often keep repeating the same problems and have such trouble learning from experience. We now know that their behaviors are not the result of moral failings or signs of lack of willpower or bad character— they are caused by actual changes in the brain. (pp. 2-3)

Kurt was fighting a battle complicated by his brain injury. His confusing, illogical, out-of-touch-with-reality behavior can be, in part, explained by the effect of the brain damage he suffered from the accident. Mixed with the other issues in his life, our lives and our world seemed out of control.

That night, about twenty firefighters stayed on the mountain to keep watch over our house and the property surrounding it, just in case any of the remaining hot spots started to be a problem. I was grateful for the crew and for all those who had been helping and who were keeping watch over us. It was comforting to know that someone was.

The next morning, I went into our separate little guest house, which was slightly uphill from our dining room. It was a place that I would go for quiet time and where the girls and I would enjoy "camping out" on weekend nights. The boombox played our favorite songs while the girls colored, and we read late into the night, often dining on popcorn, oysters, cheese, and crackers and drinking sparkling cider.

I will never forget gazing out of the soot-glazed window, devastated by the blackened wasteland that surrounded our home. The beautiful, healthy pinion pines, sage, and desert peach that graced the side of the mountain and turned our home into a forested wonderland were all gone. The beauty and life and bountiful green were destroyed, replaced only by smoldering ash and charred bits of trees and shrubs. It looked like a burnt moonscape. The beauty was gone, and all that was left was ashes. What I saw with my eyes was exactly how I felt in my heart about our lives.

— Chapter 10 —

Truth: The Line Drawn

A couple of years later, at the prompting of my good friend Lori, I was encouraged to call Doug Weiss with Heart to Heart Ministries Counseling Center in Colorado Springs. John and Lori had become friends with Doug and his wife over the previous four or five years, as both couples attended the same church. Doug's ministry helped people, primarily men, with severe addiction issues, specifically sexual addictions. Lori was the one person who had questioned whether Kurt had an issue with pornography earlier on, and she now suggested that I call Doug to see what counsel or help he might offer.

In our phone conversation, I told Doug I truly didn't know or understand all that was going on with Kurt. In all fairness to Kurt, he had been through a lot these past seven years with his accident and head injury. I explained the increasing confusion and his erratic behavior. Doug began to ask me questions: *Do you fight?* Yes. *About what?* Sex mostly. *How often?* Nearly daily.

We talked for a long time. Although empathetic to Kurt's situation, Doug told me that I needed to find out the truth.

I replied, "How do you do that? The guy can twist a dime!"

His answer: "You need to have him take a lie detector test."

"How?" I asked. He explained that we could go down to the local sheriff's office and request one. "We can't do that—we are in a small town and know everyone." He then mentioned that we could come out to Colorado Springs, have Kurt take the test there, and we could go through a week of counseling. Well, I would have to think about it. I wasn't sure how all of that would happen, or if it even could happen. I certainly wanted to know the truth, but I just wasn't sure how we would get there.

One night, about two weeks after my phone call with Doug, I was up late working in the office. I decided to look up some information on the Internet. When I logged onto the computer, a warning message came up stating that someone on our computer had accessed an explicit pornography website. For some time, I'd noticed that Kurt had been spending a lot more time on the computer with the door closed. It hit me then that Kurt's new interest in the computer might be explained by this message. I wondered exactly how I would bring up this issue with Kurt. I did a screen print as evidence of what I had seen.

I went to bed tired. As my head hit the pillow, Kurt awoke and began to pursue me. I rebuffed him and sat up, determined. "Kurt, all these years you have been treating me terribly, calling me names, chasing me, pursuing me like an animal. We are going to talk, but we are going to talk with the lights on."

I got up, turned on the lights, and returned to our bed. I showed him the paper with the web address, and he immediately replied that the girls must have accessed that site.

"No, Kurt. The girls don't even know what this three-letter word means, and they have never used the Internet." He began to tell me that the message must have been an error. No, it wasn't a mistake. All these years, this was no mistake.

I told him briefly about Heart to Heart Ministries Counseling Center and then informed him that he had some choices to make. I needed him to take a lie detector test. If he chose not to do that, I would assume that he was guilty, and I would be leaving with the girls. It was his choice.

After a pause, he said to me, "Well, you will learn some things you don't know. But I have never been unfaithful to you." In my heart, I felt like I knew what he meant: no physical body, perhaps—no explicit "affair." But what else would be revealed—well, I thought, at least we were finally going to find out. That night there was no more fighting.

It was more than a month before we could get our week-long appointment scheduled with Doug. The night before our departure, we planned to stay at a Best Western hotel right across from the airport, since our flight left at 6:00 am. I had packed our things, and we took Allie, Emma, and Rebecca to Papa and Nunie's home.

It was mid-January, cold, but the roads were clear. The conversation in the car was icy with neither of us having much to say. We had a quick dinner in the hotel and then got to our room by about 8:00. I put my flannel nightgown on, and both Kurt and I brushed our teeth and got into bed since it was going to be an early morning.

We had barely got into bed before Kurt started making advances toward me. Really? We were heading out to Colorado Springs to find out what he was hiding, and he wanted to have sex? No, I was not interested. Kurt emphatically stated that I *was* interested, that we didn't have our kids with us, we were in a romantic hotel (*the airport Best Western?* I thought incredulously), and that we were going to have sex. I told him again that I was not interested, but he just kept pursuing me and said, "We are going to have sex!"

"Over my dead body," I said in a firm voice. But he would not stop his pursuit of me. I sat up in the bed, wanting to get up, and he literally ripped my nightgown around my neck. I immediately got up, got dressed, and left the room with my suitcase.

I drove around the city, finally stopping to call John and Lori and recount what had happened.

John said to me, "You need to get him on that plane tomorrow. Can you go back into the room?"

"Well, I'm sure he won't harm me." John suggested that if I didn't feel safe, perhaps I could rent the room next door for the night to be sure that we got on the plane. It was imperative that we both get on the plane. I decided to go back to the hotel and to the room we were staying in.

As I entered the room, Kurt was watching TV and turned it off. I didn't have anything to say to him; I sat down at the small table, exhausted. Kurt immediately said to me, "What's wrong with me?" A question he had asked me many times.

"I don't know, but I guess we're going to find out." I slept in the chair that night.

The sadness and even the anger in my heart couldn't

be shaken, but my tired body and mind made me feel more numb than anything. I was exhausted from this battle. It is never okay to force yourself on someone sexually against their will, even if you are married to them. It wasn't okay for Kurt to do that to me. And it is always right in the sight of God to resist someone who is violating your consent, even if that person is your husband. Earlier that evening, Kurt had again quoted the one scripture he often waved in my face, "Your body is not your own"—a popular verse for abusive men to use out of context to try controlling their wives—but I knew I was justified in putting a stop to his unwanted pursuit of me. In fact, it was my responsibility as a wife and a woman to not allow his abusive behavior toward me to continue. I couldn't have felt more estranged, more disconnected from Kurt than I did. As I finally drifted off to sleep around 2:30 a.m., my last thought was, *Will we really find help in Colorado?* I prayed we would.

Early the next morning, through dry eyes, I reviewed our bill as we were checking out. There was an additional fee for an adult-rated movie. So *that's* what he was watching when I came in, I thought to myself. As we turned toward the shuttle waiting outside the front doors, Kurt said, "Isn't it a shame that a married man has to resort to a movie?" Yes, isn't that a shame. I didn't have a thing to say to him.

Early the next day we met with Doug at Heart to Heart for about ninety minutes. He gave us some reading materials, and that afternoon Kurt took the lie detector test. The test results were not positive: Kurt had been lying about a lot of things. He had been viewing pornography probably three or four times per week, as well as going to men's clubs and watching Xrated films at adult "theaters." It became clear that Kurt had not been telling the truth for many years.

He tried to explain these things away, then changed tactics and said that the man administering the test "made him" say far more than he'd actually done. Good try, Kurt, but I wasn't buying it. Doug confirmed that the test results are most often accurate and trustworthy. This was Kurt's way of not taking responsibility for what he was doing. It was always someone else's fault, not his. We left for the day, and Kurt was mad. I was relieved in a way, sad in another, and numb overall. It had been a long haul to get to this point. Finally, there was some truth, some answers to our crazy world and to Kurt's behavior.

That night I read one of the books Doug had given me to read called, *An Affair of the Mind.* It was, in a way, like reading our own story. Some of the things this author described her husband doing were some of the very same things Kurt would do: for instance, sitting at a table with a spoon suspended in his mouth for a very long time, unaware of his bizarre behavior. For Kurt, it was sitting in a Sunday morning service with a pencil suspended between his teeth for many long minutes. I would nudge him, but he would give no response. Finally, after repeated nudgings and a word or two, Kurt would remove the pencil poking out from his mouth. Oh, the enemy is not tame; he wants all of the man, his mind included. In the case of this author, her husband had been reduced nearly to a "loaf of bread." I felt Kurt was not far behind him.

I learned a lot about sexual addiction during this week. I'm not sure Kurt did, or that he wanted to. What hit me most is the fact that sexual addiction is a truly powerful addiction, not unlike heroin, causing high levels of dopamine to be released in the brain. With each exposure to pornography, the brain releases this chemical, and new neuro-pathways are formed, which ultimately push the user to more frequent exposure, or exposure to more hardcore porn to get the same kind of feeling of pleasure or excitement.

Later, I read a statement by Dr. Jeffrey Satinover, a psychiatrist, psychoanalyst, and physicist with degrees from MIT, Harvard, Yale, and the University of Nice. He was speaking at a Senate hearing on the effects of pornography, specifically relating its powerful effect on the human brain: "It is as though we have devised a form of heroin 100 times more powerful than before, usable in the privacy of one's own home and injected directly into the brain through the eyes."

Continued, repeated exposure to this "accepted" evil can actually cause brain damage, affecting the frontal lobes of the brain, which is where we make sound, logical, reasonable, rational, safe, and moral choices. Is it any wonder the craziness, the distorted thinking, the abuse? Kurt had, in some ways, become like a rebellious, childish, destructive (self-destructive as well as outwardly destructive), nearly robot-like abuser of something that was going to take him down if he didn't take it seriously. I was scared for him, for our marriage, for our family.

People with sexual addiction either "act out" or "act in." One who "acts out" with their addictions often pursues other extra-marital relations, but also still pursues sexual relations with their partner— sometimes hounding her, as Kurt did me. Others who "act in" stop having any kind of sexual relationship with their partner and reject them in this area of their relationship. Either way, the addiction drives the addict's actions, with inappropriate and illicit behavior reigning and ruling them.

Often people enslaved to sexual addiction become extremely self-centered, almost narcissistic, with them and their needs being the only thing that matters to them. I realized I was just a "fix" for Kurt, and that was the reason he treated me like a non-person. Sadly, women are often reduced to the sum of their body parts, seen only as objects by the men who view the fantasy and filth of porn. Women are used and abused. How can it not wreck our marriages and our families? It is wrecking our world today as surely as it was wrecking my family.

We received great counsel from Doug during that week on how to build a relationship and real intimacy, and how to build and restore our marriage. It would start with honesty: Kurt would have to be honest with himself, honest with God, and honest with me. Then there was the need for accountability and getting help for the addiction. Doug recommended the group SAA (Sexual Addicts Anonymous) and consistent counseling with a counselor or pastor.

At the end of the week, Doug met with Kurt and me separately, then together. To me, Doug said that he didn't see Kurt really wanting to change, to face the truth, and to get help. He hoped he was wrong. For me, he said that I would need to decide what I wanted for my life. It would be apparent in these next weeks and months if Kurt was at all interested or sincere in getting help. If Kurt wasn't going to work—and it would take an all-out commitment on his part to deal with these problems—then I had to decide what I must do for my sake and for our girls. We left with instructions to "date," resources to help us learn to communicate better and build our relationship, and some tools to face the monster in our world. Kurt was to join the closest SAA group and get accountability in his life.

We left and, in all honesty, I didn't really sense that Kurt was going to take the steps necessary to get help. He was still blaming me for being "frigid," and I knew that, while he was leaving me alone at the moment, he was counting down the days until he could pursue me sexually. I think we went on one date during that first month. Kurt went to one SAA meeting in Reno and came back saying he didn't really want to go. He didn't go again. John had offered to help him with the accountability issues in his life, but that didn't happen either.

I continued to pray for the Lord's wisdom and direction, crying out to God to help us, to save our marriage, and to heal Kurt. I poured out my heart to God on paper, sharing my deepest thoughts and greatest prayers for our family, for His will to be done.

In contrast to Doug's wise counsel, after returning from our week in Colorado Springs, both Kurt and I went separately to see the pastor of the church we attended. When I mentioned the issue of pornography addiction, the pastor seemed somewhat empathetic but immediately stated, "Many men deal with that issue. Not at all uncommon in the church, even." Nothing else was said for a few minutes.

A bit confused by his lack of follow-up, I was wondering if his thinking was that it—pornography use and addiction—was okay? He went on to say that he, and the church, believed that a woman—even in the case of physical abuse—was not to leave her husband, quoting 1 Corinthians 7:10 (even though the passage did not address abusive relationships). Now, I was confused.

I politely remarked, "Bob, if either your wife or your daughter were in an abusive situation, I'm sure you wouldn't counsel them to stay."

I'll never forget his reaction. He moved to the edge of his seat and said forcefully, "Don't you ever, ever bring up my wife or my daughter in this counseling room . . . *ever!*"

I obviously hit a nerve. That session didn't end well. I was reminded by a wonderful pastor a few weeks later that Bob hadn't finished this important passage: ". . . the wife should not leave her husband . . . *but if she does leave,* she must remain unmarried, or else be reconciled to her husband . . ." (emphasis mine). God's way, rightly and compassionately, provides a way "out." His way gives protection and provision for a woman who needs such help.

In the months following, life did not get better. In fact, in some ways, it got worse. A year after going to Colorado, I told Kurt that if he chose to get help and pursue the things that Doug had counseled him to do in the next month—if I saw him make an effort to get help and save our marriage—I would stay. If I didn't, I would be separating from him. The girls and I would move to town.

One early morning with Kurt once again waking me up at 4:00 for sex, it was as though I saw a line drawn down the center of our bed. At that moment I knew I had three choices: stay without standing up for myself, and go crazy; stay while fighting for respect Kurt refused to give me, and one of us might kill the other; or leave with a little bit of sanity left and a tiny bit of energy to raise our girls. The decision was clear.

Part Three
Wandering

— Chapter 11 —

Leaving for Now

Leaving Kurt—separating from my husband—was perhaps the hardest thing I have ever done. It had taken years to figure out what was truly happening to him. And even after the truth was revealed in Colorado, it still took me another year to finally raise the "white flag" in my heart and surrender. I never thought it would go this way. I had all those promises, remember? "Did I not tell you if you believe, you will see the glory of God?" I had one job: to believe God for the things He had shown me, right? I had held onto that anchor for almost eight years now, and God had to peel my hands off of it. I was worn to a frazzle, nearly having lost my own health and sanity before I finally let go. I knew when the line was finally drawn and it was finally time to leave. For me, for Kurt, and—most importantly—for our girls, it was time to separate for a while.

Our girls needed one of their parents to be sane, to be there for them and raise them as a parent should. It was apparent that Kurt was spiraling down, and I wasn't willing to go with him. Our girls needed me, and raising them alone was much better than the crazy world our lives and home had become. In some ways, dealing with Kurt was more difficult than raising a child.

Our girls were still young, but old enough to know that what was happening around them wasn't good. Allie turned twelve the weekend before I moved out in February of 2002; Emma was ten, and Rebecca was eight. These were very formative years for our girls, and I wasn't willing to compromise their well-being for anything, not even our marriage. The constant fighting and arguing, the anger, the resentments, the lack of peace and honesty and truth and respect—everything that makes a good home was missing.

I was completely and totally worn out by the years of fighting and could never have made the move without help. Thankfully I still had several faithful friends willing to step up once again to the ugly plate of my life and help me move. Tina and Jeannie, the most treasured friends I could have ever asked for, came to my rescue and helped pack and load and unload and move the girls and me to our rental house in town. They were there like sisters, through thick and thin, never letting go of my girls and me. They loved us, and they loved Kurt too, but they knew I could no longer just stay. Something had to give, or I wasn't going to make it, which would mean our girls wouldn't make it. And that wasn't an option.

It was difficult going through the process of what to take and what to leave. I didn't want to take everything, just what we needed, because I believed we would be back. Should I take our bedroom set or leave it for Kurt? It was ours—not mine, not his. How could I be making these decisions? It was all ours. Not his. Not mine.

Our world had been divided and broken before, but now it was physically divided in two in every way. His closet, his room, his home. My closet, my room, my home. I left the master bedroom set for him and took another set for me. Take this sofa, leave that one—but rearrange it all, so it still looks nice for him. Take these pictures for me, leave the outdoor pictures up for him. Enough dinnerware for me and the girls, enough for Kurt.

Difficult choices, difficult decisions. But what else do you do when you are pushed to the wall to survive? You choose. You make choices you never thought you'd be making. There are no "good" choices, really; certainly, no "right" choices. You do the best you can. You just have to survive. Numbly for now, but— especially for your kids' sake—you will survive. I knew I had to do what I had to do.

Kurt knew we were moving out that day. I had told him that if I saw him make some effort to get help and face the issues honestly, I would stay to work things out. If I didn't see any attempt on his part, then I would be moving out in a month. No effort was made. In fact, things seemed to intensify and get worse. It had been a year since we had gone to Colorado, and things only continued to unravel in our lives.

It was during this month-long waiting period that my friend Celine called me. I was doing errands in town while the girls were at the dance studio when she called.

"Shawn, are you covering for Kurt?"

I replied, "Well, I'm not sure what you are referring to—I certainly don't talk to many people about Kurt, just my few trusted friends—but, no, I'm not 'covering' for him." She then went on to tell me that she had just left the grocery store where she'd had an interesting conversation with a friend who had some information that I should know about.

This woman had mentioned to Celine (who was going through a separation) that she was sorry to hear that her friend—the one married to the building contractor with three little blonde girls—was also getting a divorce. This woman thought I had moved out and had some information that I needed to know. Celine didn't want to try and explain it; she said she wanted me to hear it directly from this woman. She told me I could find her as she worked in the card section of the store, and that her name was Caroline.

I went into the store and searched down a couple of aisles before seeing a woman about my age. I approached her, asking if she was Caroline. "Yes, I am."

"I think that you have some information that I need to know."

Yes, she did.

She went on to explain how, about a week or so ago, she had overheard this man talking in a loud voice to another man and his wife or girlfriend. The man's voice was very loud and agitated; it almost seemed like he had been drinking or something. When she saw the man, she recognized him as having attended her church a few years back. The same Baptist church we had been attending at the time.

She said this man was saying how his wife was this weird homeschool mom who had left him and taken his kids away from him. He was talking so loudly that the other man just kept saying, "It's gonna be okay, Kurt." The woman kept circling the aisle, as they both seemed nervous with Kurt's agitated state.

Kurt went on to tell this man how I didn't like sex and that he was sick and tired of it. He had been reunited with an old girlfriend, and he had just decided to "go for it" with her.

"Could this be your husband?" Caroline asked me. Yes, that was surely my husband, and it was obviously me whom he was talking about. I told her that I had not left him or our home and, no, I hadn't taken his children away from him.

"What about the other woman?"

"I don't know. I don't really think it's true. Perhaps in his mind . . . but then again, anything is possible."

I left feeling somewhat humiliated and embarrassed. Kurt had "stripped me naked" many times before, in front of many people, and I was somewhat numb to it by now. Just kind of tired and worn out by all the craziness. Would it ever end?

I waited for several days to see if Kurt would perhaps, by a really long shot, bring up this conversation with who-knows-who he had been talking to that night. Of course, he didn't, and on that next Saturday morning as Kurt was eating his cereal, I decided to bring it up. I wanted to determine exactly what he had said and if there was, in fact, this "other woman."

"Kurt, I just wanted to talk to you about a conversation that you had with someone recently. You told them that I had left you and taken the girls away from you."

"I don't know what you are talking about," he stated, staring straight ahead.

I went on to recount what he had said: that he was sick of not having sex and that he had been in touch with an old girlfriend and had decided to "go for it" with her.

"I don't know what you are talking about!"

"Well, would you like me to jog your memory?" No comment. "How about Raley's, the card aisle, last week?"

"I don't know what you are talking about! Someone is trying to break us up! They know we are having trouble and they just want to break us up!" Fuming, he continued, "Who was it? Was it Tina? Was it Celine?"

I told him, no, it wasn't either of them, and it didn't matter anyway. He got up, continuing to insist that "someone" was trying to split our (very broken) marriage apart. Someone, but not him. He was angry, agitated, and thoroughly mad at me. He walked out abruptly, saying again how I always had to wear the pants in the family. I thought to myself, *You are absolutely lying to me, and you can only twist this into me trying to "wear the pants" in the family?* Crazy. Yes, he could twist a dime.

Within a few minutes, he came back into the house and found me in the office. He said the person who told me must have mistaken him for someone else.

"No," I said, I knew it was him from the bizarre conversation, the phrases "homeschooler," "no sex," "left him" . . . "No, no mistake, Kurt. It was you."

About thirty minutes later, he came back in again. Okay, he knew what this person had overheard: He had seen a friend, Ted, who had had an affair with another friend's wife some years back. Well, he and Ted were talking about Kathy, and Kurt said that he too had a crush on her. So that's what this person heard. No, I still didn't buy it. At this point, it didn't really even matter. Nothing could be more messed up, more confusing and crazy, than our marriage.

The next weekend I caught him in another lie when he went into town. He wasn't really where he said he was. Even though he knew I had given him notice that I would be leaving unless I saw some effort and commitment on his part to seek help, his actions and behavior were getting more out of control.

It was, for me, time to go.

The day we moved, I had hoped that he'd show up and make an attempt to reconcile, to say he really wanted us to stay, and to indicate that he would do whatever it took to get help and to keep us. He didn't. Deep down I knew he wouldn't. His habit was to absolutely ignore even the most important happenings in his life, to deny what was going on.

Even his family leaving couldn't shake him into action and cause him to do whatever it took to make us stay. He just couldn't be honest with himself or me. Like he had always said, he would rather die than face his problems. But the problems were too big for me to ignore. I had to make some hard choices, no matter what he chose to do or not do.

Tina helped pack us up in Smith Valley. As the movers loaded the last things into the van, I thought, *Is this really it?* I couldn't believe this was my life. As I headed over the pass coming out of Smith Valley, Jeannie called. She would be waiting for me at the house in town. She asked how I was doing. The lump in my throat wouldn't let me talk. I think she could sense the tears streaming down my cheeks. Finally, the only word that I could get out was, "No."

Tina had taken our girls for the rest of the day and had them stay with her and her kids for the night. That way they wouldn't have to be a part of the painful process of moving their things into their new home. They had known that we would be moving, and I had talked openly with them about a change, about leaving for a while in hopes that things would get better between their dad and me. They were brave and seemed to know it had to happen. I was so thankful they were spending the night with Tina and her kids. The Smiths were dear friends, and their house was a second home to the girls. They would have fun and be distracted from what was happening for a time.

Jeannie met me at the door of our new home—she had food for us and was ready to work. We unloaded my Yukon and were ready for the movers when they showed up. After several hours, the moving van was unloaded, and we started the job of putting together all of the beds, bookcases, and other furniture. By the time that was done, it was getting late. I told her I would work on making up beds, putting away dishes, and so forth. But the ultimate organizer and faithful friend once again would not leave or let go: No, we would stay up through the night if we needed to and do it all together.

By four in the morning, everything was in its place for the girls, including fresh-baked cookies on the counter for when they would arrive home. Jeannie, my dear friend, along with Tina, helped bring order to my world. She had helped to make a beautiful home for us once again. I was so grateful for such friends. I wouldn't have made it without them.

I remember being tucked in the house the first night. It was stormy and very windy outside. I could see the huge pines that surrounded our small home, their large branches bending wildly in the gale. As I lay in my bed alone, I was thankful for the peace and the stillness within. The storm of our marriage had stopped—at least for the night.

In those first weeks, not many people knew that I had left. But just a week and a half after we moved, the pastor's wife approached me immediately after church. "I'm sorry, but God would never lead you to leave your husband!" she told me. Her words were stern, to say the least: *angry* would be a better description. She repeated herself, "I'm sorry, God would never lead you to leave your husband!"

Rather shocked by her abrupt confrontation, I didn't know what to say. I just stood there for a moment, trying to get my composure. She went on, "Are you in counseling?"

"Well, yes, we had been for years," I replied. She knew that.

"Well, you have three girls to think of."

"Yes, I have three girls, and that's exactly why I have left. What's going on in our home shouldn't be happening, so I've made a decision. You know," I continued, "we are probably the most screwed up people in this church, but I happen to know that we are not the only ones. You just think that by sweeping things under the carpet, pretending they are not there, they will just go away. Well, I won't pretend or stay in a situation that isn't good for any of us any longer." She tried to convince me that I was in the wrong for leaving.

I left that legalistic church that day, happy to know the girls and I would not be coming back. A week or so later, I received a letter from the pastor saying that I had left my God-given authority and covering: Kurt, as my husband, and the church—this particular church.

He accused me of being deceived by false leading. Well, he may have been "smarter" than me: he had his Ph.D. But I knew one thing for certain: Jesus, my Lord, leads me by His Spirit, day by day, step by step. I wouldn't have made it through these years without His leading, His presence and daily guiding, and His counsel through His Word.

I knew there was a reason why we never became members of that church, and I was happy not to be one.

— Chapter 12 —

His World, My Home

Before I ever separated from Kurt, Lee (my "adopted" dad) had said to me, "You know, if you separate from Kurt, you will be seen as the bad guy, the one to blame." Kurt was the local fair-haired boy, and many people were empathetic to him and his story. I already was the bad guy to many—certainly to Kurt and his family, as well as others.

Even while I was still at home, Kurt was telling some people that I had left him, taken the girls, and wouldn't let him see them. Now that I was gone, he seemed to want revenge all the more—yet he still wanted me to just "come home." During the first months, he would show up at our door (sometimes holding his crotch), yelling, "I didn't get married to be a monk! You just need to come home!"

It wasn't very long after I had moved out that I noticed a charge on our account that I didn't recognize. The amount—around $300—and vague description made me a bit suspicious. I decided to wait to see if Kurt would bring it up since he knew I would be paying the bill when it came.

Sure enough, he mentioned that there would be a rather large charge on the credit card statement. He told me how he had done a small construction job out in the middle of the state and that the charge was for truck repair. He felt bad about it, as he probably could have made it home without the repair being done out there.

I was now more suspicious and, since there was no number listed for the retailer, I decided to call our pastor, Steve, who had been counseling us in recent months. Kurt had wanted to see him after I left. I was so tired of going for counseling. It had been years, literally, of seeking help, but Kurt made it clear that it was me and "my issues," not him. I finally knew that without him being honest about his addictions, there really was no sense in my continuing to go with him regularly, but I did commit to going once a month.

When I told Steve about the charge, he recognized the name of the town. Mina is a very small town in the middle of Nevada with "nothing but a few prostitution houses." I made a few phone calls to determine that, yes, this charge was for a prostitution house. Doug Weiss' advice was to have someone else, preferably a man, confront Kurt on the matter with me present. So in the next scheduled counseling appointment, Steve started the session with the importance of honesty and how he and Kurt had agreed that without honesty, there is no marriage.

Steve then mentioned that I had found a charge on the credit card statement. Immediately, Kurt told him how he had already let me know that was for truck repair. Being gracious, Steve gave Kurt every opportunity to be honest. After three or four attempts to get Kurt to confess, Kurt finally spewed out in anger, "Okay, yeah, I went to a whore house, and if she doesn't come back home, I'm gonna go again!"

I'll never forget the look on Steve's face. It was apparent that there wouldn't be any rational, honest discussion about the real issues. In my heart, this truth rang loudly: when you are only an object, you are oh, so easily, replaced.

It wasn't long—perhaps sooner than I knew—before Kurt was dating and had numerous girlfriends—all the time telling me he loved me and wanted me to come back home. The confusion and craziness continued. In one breath, he loved me and wanted me to come back home. In the next, he was angrily threatening to try to "take the girls" away from me, or calling me frigid or other derogatory names.

About eight months after we separated, he had divorce papers drawn up. I believed it was just to force me or scare me back home, as he didn't follow up on them. I did, however, seek legal counsel to see what my options were. Because he was spending more money on who knows what, and his thinking and behavior continued to be so irrational, I tried to see if I could file for a legal separation. I hoped that would keep me from being liable for any debts or crazy behavior—drinking and driving or anything else—but there is no such protection in our state. If I wanted that protection, I would have to divorce him. I didn't want that, so it was a risk I had to take.

I continued to homeschool our girls and, initially, I handled the accounting and business matters for our construction business as well. With Kurt's crazy behavior, even his business was suffering, and he seemed to not have much work. It wasn't long before he told me that he didn't want me involved in the business. He would hire another bookkeeper.

Although I had an inward caution about the whole thing, I didn't have the energy or the desire to keep dealing with Kurt, even on a business level. All we did, it seemed, was argue. He kept telling me how stupid it was to be living in separate houses with double the bills. I just needed to come home. When I would mention that the issues weren't being dealt with, a flood of angry words and accusations would come pouring out, and sometimes I would have to push him out the door to make it stop. I had moved out to get some order and peace in our lives. Though it was better now than when we were living together, it seemed that often when he would come by, or we would talk by phone, we were still always arguing.

One night he had asked me out to dinner: a date to let me know how much he loved me. But with one word from me, a flurry of bizarre, hateful words came pouring out in the midst of this expensive, intimate restaurant. *Why was I keeping that body of mine hidden, to myself? Surely, I must be having an affair with someone else . . . . Or, was I gay?* His words, as always, cut me to my core. I wanted to sink into the floor, but there was nowhere to go. When he finally stopped, he looked at me with focused eyes and asked, "What is wrong with me?" I couldn't answer because I was still baffled myself.

Although we continued to struggle, I tried to have Kurt involved in the girls' world as much as possible, especially for holidays and special occasions. I so wanted them to have as normal a life as possible, with their mom and dad present at all of those important times. Even though I knew Kurt had girlfriends, I wanted the girls to have their dad around. We did seem to make most of the special occasions work for our daughters, whom we both loved so very much. But it was clear his world was not mine, and vice versa.

It is ironic to have someone insisting that he loves you while having other women in his world, both physically and mentally, through the pages of porn. My heart felt worn out, worn to shreds. I couldn't understand Kurt. He kept insisting he loved me, but when I thought about the pornography, and about the ways he was deceiving and abusing me . . . well, all of that mistreatment rendered the words "I love you" meaningless. He kept saying them, kept insisting they were true, but his actions were telling the opposite story. There was no congruity between his world and mine.

With our worlds separated and Kurt's constant pleas to "just come home," you would think that he would bend over backward to win me back. Instead, the counseling had stopped, the accountability never began, and the outward actions spoke clearly that he remained in a world to which I didn't belong. He often told people how he "wanted his girls back," but, in reality, he was making no sincere, concerted, truthful effort to bring us back home. There was no transparency and very little constructive conversation.

One day he stopped by, insisting again that I just come home. I told him that he kept asking me to come home, but he never came by to talk, to work things out, to check on me, see how the girls and I were doing, or to be honest about his life. He surprised me by saying, "You wanna talk? Okay, let's talk."

He came into the living room and sat down. He began by saying, "It all started when I was about twelve—about Emma's age." I was a bit confused, unsure what he was talking about or where this conversation was going. As he continued, I realized that he was, for the first time, voluntarily bring up the addiction issue. Because our young girls were all upstairs in their bedroom, I knew that they could easily hear this conversation, so I asked Kurt to go into the sunroom, which would provide privacy.

As he talked, it was almost as if Kurt was in a sort of trance, detached from what he was saying. It is hard to describe, but I can only assume that he had to go somewhere deep down inside himself to reveal what he was telling me.

"It all started when I was about twelve . . . We lived in Roseville and played ball down by the railroad tracks where a lot of hobos lived. One day, I was playing baseball with some friends, and the ball was hit and rolled inside a culvert. I ran into the culvert, picked up the ball, and picked up a magazine that was next to it. It was one of those 'girlie magazines.' I picked it up and looked at it—but that was not the problem. I went back later to get it."

It was that day that I finally felt Kurt opened his heart, to be honest about the issue. He admitted how bad it had become. He apologized for how terribly he had treated me over these years and said that he couldn't believe I stayed as long as I did. He was genuine in his comments. Then he said something that shocked me, something that I couldn't or wouldn't have even imagined him to ever have thought.

His words jolted me: "I'll tell you just how sick my thoughts had become. When you moved to town with the girls and into the rental house—well, I knew that house from top to bottom as I had worked on it many times over the years for the previous owner. I knew that no matter how well you had secured the house by locking the doors and securing the windows, I could break inside and rape you one more time."

The violence of his words—of that word, *rape*—shocked me. Even after living the past six or seven years of craziness and confusion, that word nearly knocked me to the floor. I felt sick to my stomach. I never imagined such a thought, ever. My head reeled as I tried to shake the ugly thought away from my own mind. It was sick and made me feel sick.

Before he left that afternoon, he said something else to me. "You are the only person who has ever figured me out." What a long road it had been. I was absolutely shaken by his honesty: I knew he had been entirely transparent with me for the first time, but it was a completely inappropriate confession. Kurt's confession of his thought of raping me may have lightened his own conscience, but it was a selfish and self-centered act—not indicative of concern for me, but just more concern for himself. Gaining his own "peace of mind" while robbing me of mine, his thoughtless words left me emotionally and mentally jolted. He should have made that serious confession to a counselor or pastor, a neutral third party. While Kurt unburdened his mind from a secret, it was harmful to me.

Sexual abuse and domestic violence are a serious threat, primarily for women, and also for a minority of men. In the church, teachings of forgiveness and "marriage is hard work" often get misinterpreted as "God expects you to stay with your abuser and endure a dangerous home environment." Nothing could be further from the truth. Demanding respectful treatment, safety at home, and freedom from sexual coercion is a godly thing to do, and so is drawing hard and fast boundaries if your intimate partner is violating those basic rights. Love says *No* to abuse. Separating; seeking civil and legal protection; insisting on the presence of a therapist for hard conversations; requiring that your spouse regularly see a mental health professional or otherwise demonstrate serious intent to end dangerous, addictive, or abusive behavior; even divorcing—all of these things are good in the sight of God and are acts of love. If you, dear reader, are in such a situation, know that you are not alone and that you have permission to get the help and support you need. (For more on this, turn to the appendix at the back of this book for resources and further reading.)

At the time, however, I did not decide to cut ties with Kurt, though it would have been more than acceptable if I had. The next several times I saw or talked to him, he alluded to our conversation and thanked me for hanging in there with him. I wanted to believe that things might be able to change for Kurt, for us. But nothing changed. Kurt was not around; there were no more conversations, no interest in me or pursuing truth and reconciliation, no offers of help as a husband with a family who needed him.

If there was a need for something to be fixed, or a way he could help, like always, he wasn't around. Even when our home was flooded with two-and-a-half feet of water in our crawl space from a broken pipe, he was no help. Calling him for some advice, I heard only, "Call Valley Heating." No interest in helping us. In fact, much of the time it seemed he thought if he could make it hard enough on me, perhaps I would come home. The reality: my home, my world, was not his world.

— Chapter 13 —

The End

I did not know how broken we could become. I would never have imagined, ever—until now. Grief that I cannot explain with words gripped my soul. Grief seemed my closest companion. It weighed me down like an anchor.

If you have ever experienced severe grief, you know what I mean. There is nothing you can do to relieve it; you can't make it go away, you can't wish it or even "pray it" away. Perhaps a pill might lift the fog, but the gray darkness clings to you like an unwanted wool blanket.

The dark surrounded my heart and soul and wouldn't let go. How could my marriage not work out? What about all those miracles? What about the promises? At times I wondered where God was in all of this and felt alone. Not just lonely, but very alone—abandoned. I wanted to believe Him, but it was so hard in the midst of such grief and brokenness. *Help my unbelief, O Lord. Help me. Help us. Heal Kurt. Heal our marriage.*

The fallout in our own marriage and lives may have been personal and private, but the shrapnel flung itself into the lives of those around us. For me, I felt that I was to keep our problems rather private, confiding in a few close friends and counselors. Unfortunately, I was married to someone who talked to anyone—friends, family, and even strangers—about our issues. He always gave his take on what was happening in our lives, much of which was not the truth at all but lies.

I'm not sure if it was Kurt's head injury that loosened his tongue, but he talked about and slandered me to anyone who would listen. I remember later reading an article by Janet Croner, RN, "After Brain Injury: The Dark Side of Personality Change," in which she described the subtle and even more pronounced changes in her own husband's behavior following an anoxic brain injury. Damage to various areas of the brain, including the frontal and temporal lobes (areas affected by Kurt's injury), could leave the person vulnerable to agitation, verbal attacks, and impaired impulse control, among other things. Still, this is devastating for a wife. Whether solely caused by his head injury or a combination of his determination to make me feel the "consequences" of separating from him by talking and slandering me, the result was that I certainly did not feel loved.

Kurt was charming, and his accident, injury, and recovery had only served to soften people's hearts toward him. Certainly, he attested, I had left him for no good reason. I just left with the girls. I found it interesting that not too many people ever approached me to find out my side of the story. Not many people want to "get dirty," to get involved enough to know what really might be going on.

Sadly, people take sides, even without knowing. I had people turn away from me in the church halls, get out of line at the grocery store when they recognized me in front of them, and even had one woman pack up her kids on the beach and leave when my girls and I showed up for a day of group summer fun at Lake Tahoe. It felt like I had become marked with a big D or S . . . Divorced or Separated.

Often, people just don't know what to do with you. Broken families, broken friendships . . . broken lives. It seems that there are no limits to the effects of loss and brokenness when it relates to trouble in a marriage. Not only was there a war within the gates, but there was also a war outside the gates. Naturally, this only intensified the pain, the grief, the loss.

For years, I knew that "so goes the man, so goes the marriage, the family, the community, the nation, and, yes, the world." (Of course, the same is true of women; both wives and husbands have an equally significant impact on their marriages, families, communities, and the world.) I had written this statement in my journals over and over again during those confusing years when I didn't know which end was up, or what was happening with Kurt. It is a scary place for anyone, man or woman, to have a loved one who seems out of control and you don't know why.

As wives, we are connected with our husband's heart, soul, spirit, and body—ours intertwined with theirs. Such is the way for anyone in a close, intimate relationship. It is God's design, and it was meant to be good. But when things go wrong with one person, you and your family are in a vulnerable place. Home isn't safe anymore. You can sense it with your gut and everything else in your entire being: something is terribly wrong. Even back then, before I knew about Kurt's struggle with addiction, I had a sense that we were in trouble. But I didn't know how very broken our lives would become.

Grief, especially when it comes through the back door of your own home, is a strange and foreboding companion. When the brokenness is caused by the one who is meant to be the protector of your heart and soul, the watchman on the wall for the guarding of your family's safety and well-being, it is especially sad and grievous.

Often I would think, in the midst of our trials and overwhelming grief: How can you, really, mend a broken heart? Can you ever win at this "game?" If left unaddressed and without the intentional, diligent seeking of help and healing, there are no winners in the world of pornography and sexual addiction. Men and women and their families stand to lose so much.

Never did I think that things would end the way they did. My plan, my heart's greatest desire, was for the complete restoration of our marriage and wholeness for our family. Separation was just supposed to be a temporary situation to hopefully bring about permanent, healthy change. Marriage without honesty is difficult; marriage without truth and fidelity is impossible.

Once the marriage covenant is broken, the marriage has ended. Whether it is through actual, physical infidelity—an affair or explicit relations with another person or persons—or through other kinds of infidelity that erode or entirely break trust (in our case, the pornography, the sexual abuse, the deceit), the marriage covenant has been defiled, broken. Broken vows make broken people and broken lives. But I totally believed, even through several years of separation, that Kurt would "wake up" and both want and pursue help to get his family back. We—the girls and I—were worth it, right? It didn't work out the way I had planned: my life, our lives, according to Shawn.

Things only got crazier and crazier. After two and a half years, Kurt once again insisted that I "come back home" or it was finally over. But there was no change and no intention of changing. There had been other women in his life and still were. No, I wasn't just "coming home." I told him that he had the divorce papers drawn up initially. If he wanted a divorce, he would have to go down and sign the papers. If he did, I would follow.

Long story short, he did. I followed.

I was somewhat surprised when my attorney's office notified me that Kurt had signed the next day. After many threats over the years, he finally did it. It was a strange feeling as I signed the documents that would officially end our marriage.

I thought I was fine, but as soon as I signed my name for the last time, on the final document, I began to cry and then to sob. I couldn't stop. The receptionist came around the desk, gave me a hug, and told me how it wasn't unusual at all: most wives who came in to sign their marriages away broke down and cried— often uncontrollably. I wasn't alone in this kind of grief. Others, many others, had paved the way. I certainly wasn't the first. Sadly, neither was I the last.

It was over. Our marriage was over. I really couldn't believe it. Once again, the miracles, the hope, the promises, all God had done for us and in our lives, flooded my mind over and over: sparing Kurt's life; performing so many miracles on our behalf; blessing us beyond measure in so many ways. It seemed surreal.

For me, it was like a death. A death of all my hopes, dreams, and expectations: not just for me, but for Kurt, for our family, and for our girls.

"Did I not tell you that if you believe, you will see the glory of God?" In some ways, that promise died too. Those words of hopeful expectation that I had clung to so often through the years no longer seemed to make sense. I felt like something in me died. And it had.

Part Four
Redemption

— Chapter 14 —

The Summer

Life continued on with our girls completing middle school and moving on to high school and college. Kurt was involved, but not much: certainly not day-to-day, when real life happens. It really was mainly the girls and me. He provided some consistent support financially, and for that, I will always be grateful. He saw the girls once a week or so, and about every other week they would spend a day together on the weekend, perhaps spending the night at his home. He was still their dad. He made them laugh. I was still their mom. I reviewed their papers, saw them through their years of dance, years of school and growing up, and helped them navigate their paths to college. We were still their parents, no matter how incomplete or screwed up we were.

Some things never change and cannot change. Some things that change *should* not change, and our kids pay the price for them. We still and always loved our girls and always will. God faithfully has provided for them and given them much, in spite of their parents. But they, too, lost out on a "whole family"—a family that stayed together through thick and thin, good and bad, in sickness and in health. A family with a mom and a dad present, united and in love, to teach them the things that parents are meant to teach them: love, faithfulness, devotion, sacrifice, selflessness, honor, and respect. Parents who would be together at their college graduations. Parents who would walk them down the aisle together at their weddings, rejoice at the births of their children, lovingly dote on all the grandchildren, and support them together throughout their lives. We always loved them, always. But we could not, with a broken marriage, a marriage that ended, give them all they were intended to have. They too have been cheated by wrong choices, broken promises, broken lives.

It seemed impossible, but time continued onwards, marching us forward. How could those years have flown by? I continued to homeschool the girls until Emma had graduated from high school. Then with Rebecca the only daughter left at home and me needing to work full-time, it was time for her to go to high school, and we decided on a private Lutheran school. A little nervous to enter into the private sector of school, we were all so proud of Becky when she graduated from SLHS with nearly a 4.0 GPA and was salutatorian of her graduating class of 2012. Tears streamed down my cheeks as Rebecca gave the most articulate, heart-warming, and candid speech that graduation evening.

I know Kurt also felt the tug on his heart-strings as a father, as we exchanged glances during her talk. He too had tears in his eyes. We had been through a lot, but we both always loved our girls and wanted the best for them. We were their parents; they were our girls. Always. Some things can't ever be changed, even by our sin and stupid choices. Once a family, always a family.

Rebecca was just a baby when Kurt was in the auto accident; one month old, and now here she was graduating at the top of her high school class. Oh, how do eighteen, twenty years fly by? It really is a mystery, this thing we call time.

Just three weeks before, Allie, our oldest, had graduated from Westmont College in Santa Barbara. I felt the same pride seeing her in her cap and gown, knowing her hard work over those four years to earn a double major in business (emphasis: economics) and communications at Westmont College, an academically rigorous institution. She, like her two sisters, is diligent, hard-working, and intelligent, but she intentionally mixed her academic pursuits with a purposed effort to get to know many people in her social worlds of college, work, and dance, to experience a variety of people and adventures, and opportunities to learn, work, and serve. Kurt was there beaming as Allie was called to receive her diplomas. So was I. Jeannie, Karen, and family—so many were there, as always, lovingly supporting our girls as they have for their entire lifetimes. Audra, the girls' beloved "Nunie," came as well with her daughter Lisa, which meant so much to all of us. How could we have made it without the love and support of such faithful friends?

With Allie now graduated from college, Emma ready to enter her third year at Loyola Marymount University, and Rebecca having graduated from high school preparing to enter Westmont College, it felt like we had reached a significant milestone in life. Again, how did that happen? Three lovely girls now raised— grown up, really—and conquering the world. It was so exciting to see them at this stage and these ages. I loved every minute of being a mom.

Taking a vacation from my finance position with a private trust company, I made plans for the girls and me to gather at a little vacation home in Laguna Beach for a week to celebrate Allie's and Rebecca's graduations and to rest and relax. I had taken a little more than a week's vacation over the Memorial Day weekend. Although we had to juggle the girls' work schedules, graduation parties and trips through the week, it was a special time to be together, the four of us girls. Our friend Sarah joined us for part of the week of laughter, games, cooking, and food, walking the beach, swimming, paddle boarding. It seemed the perfect culmination to the month's graduation celebrations. I knew in my heart that time, as we had known it together, would be changing more and more. The girls all would have their own plans, even more now that Rebecca was out of high school, Allie out of college, and Emma starting her very busy third year of college with a double major in philosophy and business. Oh, how life can change in a moment, in a day.

As we all departed, I felt a sadness that we were all going separate ways this time, except for Rebecca and me. I was certainly thankful for the time we had together; I just somehow wanted to keep all the "chicks" close in heart and at home, but really I wouldn't change their plans and direction for anything. I was so proud of our girls, so happy to see them living life to the fullest, challenging themselves, and eager to move forward to the next things.

Rebecca returned to a rigorous dance schedule that first week back, as her studio's annual performance was to be the next weekend. She also started a new job at the lake. Emma was to start work as an orientation leader with freshmen at LMU. Allie was to head off to Washington, D.C. for a conference and then back to Santa Barbara to continue working in her job there. I was to return to work at the trust company in Reno. Life was "normal" again.

Late in the night before I returned to my job from vacation, I received a phone call from Stacey, an ex-girlfriend of Kurt's who was still living at his home. She told me that Kurt was being taken by ambulance to Reno with doctors suspecting liver cancer. He had not been feeling well for perhaps quite some time but didn't go to the doctor until now. He had bile in his urine and was in some pain. They hadn't done extensive testing yet, so this was just a guess. Being late and knowing I had to leave for work very early in the morning before Rebecca was even up, I asked Stacey not to contact our girls or post anything on social media. I wanted to find out more and hopefully know something before telling them. I didn't want to alarm them without having more information.

Immediately after work, I headed to St. Mary's Hospital. As I drove up to the hospital, I thought of the three times we had been there when each of our little baby girls were born. Bringing them out into the light of day for the first time, buckling their car seats in the back seat, and heading home with precious cargo: each one of our tiny daughters. This was a special place for those miraculous moments in life that God had given us. We were so excited and blessed with each baby girl lovingly granted into our care, into our hearts and our family. Coming back now to check on Kurt drew me to a different place. What could be happening now with him and his health? I didn't want to question too much yet.

As I entered Kurt's room, he was sitting up at the end of the bed. His very first words to me were, "I know that God spared my life nineteen years ago, and for that, I am grateful because I have gotten to see our three girls grow up. And not that I don't believe that God could do it again if He wanted to. But if He doesn't, it's okay. The life I've lived for the past ten years has been no life at all."

Just seeing him there once again in a white gown, vulnerable and honest, made me realize the deep connection we still had despite all the hard years and trials.

I asked if they knew yet what was wrong, and he said they had been doing testing on him throughout the day; but, as of yet, things were inconclusive: no answers, but very possibly cancer. I asked him how long he'd not been feeling well, and he responded, "You know me, I just ignore things and work." *True*, I thought. For Kurt, it could have been months that he really didn't feel well. Even he wasn't sure. Somehow as we talked, we kind of knew this might be "it"—that the end of the road might be near. Don't know why or how, but it seemed like we were both being prepared. We talked about the girls, how proud we both were of them. How delightful they are. Somehow it just seemed right that I was there.

In the midst of our talk, Kurt stopped and then asked me, "If it would make it easier on you, I would ask you to marry me again."

I knew he was sincere. "Kurt, I'm not sure if that is the right thing to do," I said. Pausing for a moment, I added, "I do know that no one can ever take away all that we have been through together." Trying to hold back the tears, we prayed together for the first time in a very long time. Somehow in the light of our troubles now, the troubles of the past, the trials, the hurt, all seemed to be washed away. This was my girls' dad, my husband for many years. Once again, we were put together to enter into another storm that we didn't know anything about.

Kurt mentioned getting things in order; I would be handling his affairs for him, for our girls. I didn't really want to talk about that then, but he seemed to need to. I ended up staying for a couple of hours that late afternoon but didn't get to see any of the doctors. I had tried to call Rebecca several times to see how her rehearsal was going, to check on her, but she didn't call me back. As I left the hospital, I was a bit concerned about her and wondering why she wasn't calling me.

Stacey had called to check on Kurt and mentioned that she had talked to Rebecca earlier. Not realizing that Rebecca didn't know yet, Stacey accidentally "updated" her on Kurt's condition. I was upset now, knowing that Becky had found out about her dad while up at her rehearsal; she must have been in such turmoil, not knowing the facts. I left to go find her. She still wasn't returning my calls. By the time I got home, she was there—naturally in tears and upset. She cried in my arms. My tears silently drenched her precious little head. I wasn't even sure what to tell her.

The next days were difficult, trying to decide when to call Allie and Emmie. We still didn't know much. The multiple tests for cancer were conflicting: some indicated cancer, others didn't. However, the GI doctor seemed fairly certain that it was cancer—cancer of the liver, perhaps—but he too was a bit perplexed by the tests. I was wondering what exactly to tell our girls. Should they come home? What do I tell them? We didn't know anything for certain, but I sensed the seriousness of Kurt's condition. Once again, as it had been after Kurt's accident, it seemed a matter of life and maybe death for Kurt, but this time our girls were older, grown, really. In some ways, this time it seemed harder. So much more to consider for their sakes now.

When I called the older girls, Emma made plans to drive up that next night after work; Allie was flying back from D.C. on Thursday night and ended up driving through the night to make it up early Friday morning. They each wanted to see their dad. They both wanted to be there for Becky's dance recital on Friday and Saturday nights. They had always, all three, been together for these events. I was so thankful that they were as close—truly close as sisters and as friends—as they were. Homeschooling had allowed many things in our lives: being close as a family with flexibility in our world; allowing our girls to spend enormous amounts of time together; sharing every aspect of their lives; building not just moments and memories, but relationships that would stand the test of time and trials in this life. This had been another great gift to us. They would need each other through this time. We all would.

When Allie and Emma arrived at the hospital, Kurt was in severe pain. Although he tried initially to push back the pain, as he so wanted to visit and catch up with the girls, he just couldn't. The doctors gave him pain medication to tolerate the discomfort—which, given Kurt's usual tolerance, told me how bad the pain must have been. (We learned later that the doctors had accidentally nicked his pancreas during a test.) It was hard to see him wrestle with trying to be brave, strong for the girls, and be vocal about how he was really feeling. Certainly, Kurt was never one to complain when his body hurt. It was hard for me. I'm sure it was incredibly hard for our girls.

This was the beginning of our summer.

Chapter 15

Truths and Full Circles

It was now the third week in July, and Kurt was back in the hospital for exploratory surgery and to hopefully determine what else was going on. He had finally been diagnosed just a week earlier with colon cancer. The doctors knew now that he had a malignant tumor in his colon, perhaps causing some of his pain. We had been in this same hospital, Washoe Medical Center, just weeks earlier on July 5th when Emma and I went with Kurt to an appointment with a surgeon. On that day, while getting a tour of the cancer center, I received a call from my brother: my sister's husband had just died suddenly, apparently from a heart attack. Her world, their world, was just turned upside down. How could this be? Mike was only fifty-four years old, and my sister only forty-nine. I went into work to wrap things up and make plans to fly out to Connecticut late that night.

The next weeks seemed surreal in many ways, watching my younger sister and her two young adult children in shock, grieving Mike's passing. It was so painful to watch, to watch their pain and suffering, to see their great grief. I was glad to be there with them all, to share in this difficult time. There is no "good time" to die, no time when we are fully prepared to say goodbye to the ones we love. There is One, though, who has numbered our days, and He alone knows that number, for each one of us. To me, that is a great comfort. Our lives are under His sovereign control, even though we may not understand our circumstances.

After a difficult but beautiful celebration of Mike's generous, kind, and loving life, I returned to our home in Nevada. I knew for my sister and her kids that life would never return to "normal" again. I was thankful that Mike had been the man he was, and that Chris and her children would grieve (and grieve greatly, for perhaps a very long time), but they had the memories and the foundation of a faithful husband and dad to anchor them for the rest of their days. Mike's life, in some ways, would live on through theirs. They had been blessed to have had him, though the years were cut too short. We were surely all blessed to have known him.

I returned home to a diagnosis: yes, Kurt did have colon cancer, a malignant tumor. The doctors scheduled an exploratory surgery early the next week. Rebecca planned to drive her dad to the hospital that day, and I would leave work and meet up with them there. Just before leaving the hospital, Rebecca called. "Mom, Dad was in so much pain he asked me to pull over and call for an ambulance." They were just south of Reno. I could hear her voice quiver, but she insisted she was okay and would meet me at the hospital. I knew Kurt must be in great pain to have her stop and call for help.

We arrived in the ER at the same time that Kurt was being brought in. It seemed that Kurt was having difficulty processing what was going on, thinking he was there for surgery, not sure why he was in the ER. He finally made it out of ER just in time to make his surgery on the third floor.

Just before leaving the ER, Jane—one of Kurt's girlfriends—made her way into the room, large duffel in hand, apparently wanting to share the journey. I didn't really know the status of Kurt's "dating life" at that time, but I had seen her once with him at a dance recital. The girls never mentioned she was still around. Rebecca seemed surprised to see her.

As Jane put her belongings in the corner, Kurt looked me directly, quietly saying, "I'm sorry, Shawn, I didn't know she was coming."

We were rushed to the pre-op room, an aide wheeling Kurt in a wheelchair. The nurses gathered Kurt's clothes and handed them to me. Jane kept kissing Kurt, which increased the awkwardness of an already strained situation. The doctors had told us the procedure would take an hour and a half to two hours.

Hungry by now, Becky and I talked about finding a restaurant in the hospital. Jane asked if she could come along. We had an interesting conversation. Asking her about herself and what she did, she mentioned that she was an artist. When I asked her what type of artwork she was into, she pulled her laptop out of her bag. She had made a present for Kurt: a rather strange picture taken from the Avatar movie, with a huge winged dinosaur-like creature and a half-man, half-creature on its back.

"Do you recognize someone?" she asked Rebecca and me.

We both looked again, then, looking at each other, said, "No."

"It's Kurt," she said, pointing at the creature's human face. "Recognize him now?"

No, we never would have recognized him! Becky and I nudged each other beneath the table, trying not to laugh. Having her here with us at this time was so strange. I could sense Rebecca's uneasiness. In my heart, I felt like she was intruding, especially hearing Kurt say he hadn't invited her here.

We made our way to the Starbucks lounge to wait for the surgeon's phone call. It was nearly three hours after they took Kurt in. The news was not good. The surgeon confirmed the tumor was blocking the colon, and they would be going back in tomorrow to open up the passageway. He had cancer, spread like "buckshot" throughout his abdomen. He perhaps had liver cancer as well.

I asked the doctor how bad the cancer was. Stage 4, he said.

"What does that mean? Months?"

Six months, perhaps, maybe longer with treatment. He wasn't sure. He mentioned that they might need to do a colostomy at some point. I told him that Kurt might well not want to do that and that they would need to have that discussion with him if it did seem necessary down the road.

I hung up, my mind swirling, trying to think how and exactly what to tell Rebecca at this point. As I told her the news—that yes, Dad had cancer, including colon and abdominal cancer—the look in her face and the tears in her eyes told me that was enough information for now. We hugged each other as tears streamed silently down both our faces.

Kurt was scheduled for surgery at 9:00 a.m. the next morning. Rebecca had a dance rehearsal in Tahoe, so I headed into Reno, wanting to be there to see Kurt before he went back in for surgery. His very best friends, Rob and Ray, had traveled down from Wyoming, getting into Reno late the night before. They wanted to see Kurt; it had been several years since they had seen him. Little Ray came to the hospital too, and as I walked into the pre-op room, it was a comfort to see all three of Kurt's best friends surrounding him. Jane was there, too—she had apparently spent the night at the hospital hotel.

She kissed his forehead several times, which again ratcheted up my sense of tension and strangeness. If Kurt hadn't invited her, why hadn't he asked her to leave? When Jane turned away at one point, Rob shrugged his shoulders and pointed to her, mouthing the words, *Who's this? Stacey?*

No, I mouthed silently back, *Jane.*

Both Rob and Ray gave me a look like, "Who is that???" Of course, that wasn't the time to explain, if there ever would be one. Hard to explain something like that to your ex-husband's best friends, who never really knew the whole story either. Stacey had been the woman living at the house with Kurt on and off for the past few years. They didn't even know about this one . . . about "Jane." I'm not sure they knew anything much about the many others, either.

It was good to have his old, best friends around. They were making jokes—or trying to, at least—and Kurt, of course, made us all laugh with some of his remarks. I could see the concern in his friends' faces, but they once again were there as brave soldiers to stand guard as their friend faced another challenging time in his life. It was reminiscent of those long days and nights, those weeks after Kurt's accident. Here we were again. I felt a closeness to these three faithful friends, and I could see their struggle seeing Kurt now in a very tenuous state. What was the prognosis, really? We didn't know yet.

Before they took Kurt away to the surgery room, we all prayed together, once again, for Kurt, for the Lord to look after him during the surgery, to heal him. The prayers and the people were all familiar, except for Jane. She seemed out of place, and I think even she felt it.

As we all waited, it was good to catch up with Rob and Ray and what was happening with their families. Both these men had come to know the Lord during the time that they all worked together with Kurt. I could see a gentleness in both of them that years of life's weathering had worn into their characters. Not that it wasn't there before, but it seemed deeper now, as perhaps it is with all of us as we experience the difficulties of real life down here on earth. The Lord faithfully conforming us into His image.

I was so glad all three of these special men were here. For Kurt and for me. They had been my heroes during those many months and years after Kurt's accident. We needed them so, back then. We needed them again right now.

They inquired about Jane, who she was, how long she had been in the picture. I didn't know much to share: just that he had apparently been seeing her for a year or so since she had come to Rebecca's recital. Ray mentioned how Kurt seemed to relax when I came into the pre-op room; it was like he was relieved to have me there. It felt right to be there, too.

As we waited in the balcony area near the surgery center, Stacey, the other girlfriend, called me to check on how things were going with Kurt. Was he out of surgery? Did we know anything yet? She was at Kurt's house and indicated that she would come up if it weren't for Jane being there. It was then that I learned of the battle between the two of them. Stacey claimed Jane, a prospective client of Kurt's, had broken up their relationship—though it was unclear to me why Stacey was still living at Kurt's house if this was the case—and Stacey would have nothing to do with Jane. There was obvious disdain in her voice. I was glad this was not my war; I was just the ex-wife. Yet I struggled a bit in my own way. Perhaps I was the ex-wife, but I had also been the wife for so long, and this was my girls' dad.

Hours later after surgery and back in his room, Kurt had just woken. With his eyes fixed on me, he extended his hand toward me, beckoning me to take it. With tears in his eyes and an urgency in his words, he said, "I've always loved you, and I always will. My life's greatest regret is that I didn't treat you the way that I should have . . . I should have helped you more."

As these words came out of Kurt's mouth, Jane got up from the sofa that she had parked herself on for days now and quickly left the room. Rebecca, who had been sitting numbly on the sofa beside this near-stranger, was looking up now.

Taking Kurt's hand, I slid to the chair beside his bed. His eyes were genuine, full of pain. I motioned to Becky to come over, to sit with us. She came and sat down on my lap, lowering her little head onto her dad's chest. For the first time in days, and with her dad, she began to cry. Kurt lovingly stroked her hair with his big, work-worn hands. Finally, she could let go. We were alone, and she could be herself. She cried, her dad's hands, his touch, bringing comfort to her grieving heart. Tears wanted to stream down my face as I saw our youngest daughter struggle with her own pain.

Suddenly, Jane came back into the room, picked up her bag, and stomped to the door, leaving in an obvious huff. I gently slipped Rebecca into the chair to stay near her dad and headed out into the hallway.

Jane was still standing there. "It's just kind of weird," she said, obviously upset.

Nodding, I looked her straight in the eyes. "It probably is a bit weird. But once you are a family, especially when you have children, you are always a family."

Jane agreed, "I believe that." She admitted to me that Kurt had told her when all this came down in June that he had always loved me and always would. I wondered why she was still here knowing that. "In fact," she said, "I believe that all this started when you left." She circled her stomach with her hands, meaning Kurt's cancer.

"Perhaps," I said. "But Kurt doesn't have long." I could tell it was a bit of a surprise to her to finally hear this, to get it. "It's about Kurt and about our girls now, Jane. Our God is a God of full circles and restoration, and I believe that He wants to do a complete healing in our family."

She nodded and heard me. She turned and walked away. I assumed, then, that she would leave.

Rebecca and I visited with Kurt a while longer, but it was obvious that he was extremely tired. We told him to sleep, and we left the hospital for a drive. Ending up at the university campus, we parked the car and slept. It had been a long, weary week, and we had been driving back and forth between the hospital and home each day.

Returning to the room that night about 8:30, we were both surprised to see Jane was back in the room. Why? Allie and Emma both called me, saying, "Mom, Becky doesn't want her there. We don't want her there. Dad told her he still loved you when he first got sick . . . Why is she still there?"

My friend Marsha also called, questioning why this "other woman" would not leave. "Shawn, you need to be careful," she said. "You and Kurt have worked too hard all your lives to let someone else come in at the end and perhaps try to take things that belong to your girls. It happens all the time." I hadn't really thought about it like that. Getting rid of someone unwelcome can be difficult sometimes, even when it is obvious it's time to leave.

Rob, Ray, and Little Ray continued to hang out over the next day or two. They too sensed the gravity, the seriousness of Kurt's condition and wanted to help. What could they do to help us right now? I mentioned the concern with Jane not leaving and wondered if we should change the locks at Kurt's house. Stacey had mentioned something in our phone conversation about not wanting to leave the house for fear that Jane would come in while Kurt wasn't home. We talked about the girls not wanting her here. They talked with Kurt. He didn't want her there, either.

Kurt had made it clear. She was gone the next day. Finally. It was over. I was thankful for Rebecca and our other girls. They had enough on their hearts dealing with all that was going on with their dad. Honestly, my own emotions were on a rollercoaster. I was thankful she was gone so our own family could walk this journey together: for me, without another woman in the picture.

The next day, Ray and Rob had to leave for home in Wyoming as they needed to return to work. But on their way, they took the time to travel quite a distance in the opposite direction just to change the locks on Kurt's house—faithful friends to the end.

That same day, Kurt was being bombarded by two of the doctors with the proposition to go ahead with chemotherapy while he was still at the hospital. Even though he had multiple cancers, stage 4, at this point the oncologist and the surgeon pushed him to take advantage of the treatment. It would be convenient, they said.

I approached the GI doctor later that day in the hallway, mentioning the other two doctors' push to do treatment. He looked in my eyes with sincere compassion in his own. "Because I care about you and your family, I will tell you exactly what I would tell anyone of my own family members if they were in Kurt's situation. I would not recommend anything that might perhaps, *perhaps*, extend their life for a few weeks or maybe even a few months, if it was going to cause them to be sicker and maybe even more compromised for the rest of their days. It would not be worth it."

I had my answer to the treatment question more confirmed in my mind. Kurt would have to make up his own.

I told him what his GI doctor had told me. Kurt said again that he had never thought he would do any kind of cancer treatment but that somehow, now, he felt like he had to fight. I remembered him saying that very thing many times while we were married: He was never going to be that bald-headed man sitting on the couch, unable to work. No, he wouldn't, I believed. But today, I agreed that he had to do what was right for him now in his own heart.

— Chapter 16 —

Heavenly Healing

The next day Kurt committed to doing "one treatment" while he was in the hospital, just to try. Allie had come in from Santa Barbara; Emmie was on her way. They transferred Kurt from the main hospital to the cancer ward on the basement level.

Ted, Kurt's brother-in-law, had called the day before, saying that he and Meg wanted to come to see Kurt. He mentioned that Kurt's parents would be coming too. Hesitating and nearly apologizing, he awkwardly mentioned that it would probably not be good if I were there, for Kurt's parents, especially his mom. I obliged his request, of course, as I didn't want their visit to be hindered or awkward in any way.

Somehow, I had always been to them like the "other woman" in their son's life: an unwanted intruder to their family. I still was, even now. Funny—sad, really—how some things seem not to be able to change. You often cannot change someone else's opinion of you. In the end, it doesn't really matter. It has been what it has been all these years. It is still what it is. I was truly okay with that. It was just important for them to see Kurt, and for him to see them.

Through the rest of that day, we spent time together as a family. Kurt and I, for some reason, re-counted many of the events and miracles that happened now nearly twenty years ago relating to his accident. Many of the things we spoke of that day our girls had never heard us share, at least not together. They were all babies, toddlers, when Kurt had his accident. And they had only been eight, ten, and twelve when we separated.

Some of the stories they had never heard or didn't remember: the vision, the prayers, the help of so many people in our lives. God sparing their dad's life, reviving him, resurrecting him from a coma, and bringing him back from near-death to life. The people who were affected by the situation, who were changed as they walked alongside us during those weeks and months and even years. It seemed surreal that we were all gathered around his bed now, our girls all grown women.

Again, time seemed not to exist. It was standing still for us. Visits we should have had together through these lost years—somehow they seemed right and good now, restored to us in this strange time. It was the way it should have been all along. We had today. Together . . . today. Once a family, always a family. The girls took turns snuggling on the bed next to their dad. We talked a lot through the day.

The oncologist came in late that afternoon to explain the chemotherapy treatment to the girls, to us; it would hopefully kill the cancer but would also knock down Kurt's immune system, though with the hope at the end of building him back up little by little. *How long did he think this process might take?* I inquired skeptically. Six months or so. *Kurt probably didn't have six months,* I reminded this doctor who had told me

Kurt had stage 4 cancer. He laughed nervously, raising his chin high, then left the room.

To me, it didn't make any sense. Emma and Becky were both crying quietly, trying to control the tears, but they couldn't hold them back any longer. I knew Allie was trying to make sense of it all; I could see the wheels of her mind spinning, trying to grasp the weight of the situation. Life sometimes doesn't seem fair. At this moment, that was how it seemed: unfair and even cruel.

The next morning, while at work for a few hours, I received a garbled voice message from Kurt. Something about the treatment being canceled. I left work and headed to the hospital.

When I entered Kurt's room, the oncologist was there explaining that late the night before he was reading the pathology report (*hadn't he read it before now? I wondered*) and found that Kurt also had pancreatic cancer. He mentioned that he had spent hours during the night talking with other physicians who were much more familiar with treating complex, multi-cancer patients.

These doctors in Reno had never seen a patient with cancer in so many different organs at one time. They had canceled Kurt's treatment for today. It was a good thing that they hadn't started the "wrong treatment," now knowing that he also had pancreatic cancer. I shuddered to imagine the consequences if they had given him the wrong treatment for three months or more.

Later, after consulting with these other oncology experts, Kurt's doctors came up with a new treatment plan: they would give Kurt the same treatment as before but add an even more toxic treatment (their very words) to fight pancreatic cancer. Somehow, this really didn't make sense. They were going to be adding more toxic chemotherapy on top of the "wrong treatment?"

Kurt listened politely as the doctor began to explain the starting of this new regiment for fighting the enemy within his body. Finally, Kurt politely interrupted the doctor, saying that he "just needed one more reason not to do the treatments." He said he appreciated the doctor's information but that he just wanted to go home and be with his girls. Reluctantly, the doctor left the room. The decision was final. Even so, both the surgeon and oncologist returned one more time, when I had returned to work briefly, to try to talk Kurt into the treatment. No. His mind was made up.

I had to go back to work, but before we all left, the oncologist came into Kurt's room. If he was going to be leaving the hospital, it was imperative that we contact hospice—don't wait. His words were so emphatic.

Emma and Rebecca took Kurt back home to Smith Valley that afternoon. Allie returned to Santa Barbara for work. I went into the office to try to catch up.

That day, Kurt mentioned that he knew someone, a friend, who worked with hospice in Reno. (Actually, this woman was the wife of Kurt's attorney who drew up our divorce papers. Small world, really.) He would give her a call. Kurt called me at work to tell me that he had talked to Ellen. He said something about not being able to get hospice out to Smith Valley, but that Ellen would see about making an exception in his case.

As I drove into my driveway, I heard the Lord speak to my heart, "Go, measure your room for a medical bed." I knew what He was asking me to do. *Bring Kurt home.* I immediately went into my bedroom and realized that, yes, a medical bed would fit.

I went outside and sat down on the front steps and began to cry—not because I didn't want Kurt there. I did. Somehow when the end is near, nothing else really matters. I cried out from my heart, *"God, did I do the wrong thing all those years ago? Should I not have separated from him?"*

His response was quick and certain, "No, I took that marriage from you." In His grace once again, He assured me that it wasn't my doing to end our marriage. I knew in my heart that yes, of course, I would want to have Kurt here, with his girls where it was safe—home, with us. All of us. The last chapter of our lives, it seemed, was unfolding. My heart grieved the losses in those moments all over again.

Later that evening, I called Ellen and introduced myself. She began to tell me the options Kurt might consider since hospice would not extend their services into Smith Valley: He could move into an apartment in town, or he could rent a trailer, perhaps, in a county where the hospice nurses could visit him.

I felt the same kind of defensiveness and protectiveness that I felt after Kurt's accident and a head injury when the doctors wanted to send him away for perhaps three or four months to a rehab home in the Bay Area. At that time, we had three little babies under the age of four, and Kurt needed to know he had a family who loved and needed him, just as he needed us. This time was no different. No, he would stay with us.

She paused, seeming confused. "Well, I know that you and Kurt are divorced. Wouldn't that be difficult?"

"No, we have had our tough times, for sure, but I still care for Kurt. He is our girls' dad. I don't want him living in a trailer somewhere by himself. He belongs with us. We will all gladly take care of him." She was surprised, I think, but happy for the solution, happy for Kurt. I was, too. Hospice would send over a nurse in the next few days.

That night, I headed out to Smith Valley to stay with Kurt, Emma, and Becky. After a light dinner, Kurt headed to bed early. I mentioned to the girls that I thought that it might be good if Dad came to our house, to stay with us. Immediately, Emma came to her dad's defense. "Mom, Dad hates town and loves being in his shop!"

I could see the pain in her face. I assured her that they could bring their dad back and forth as much as he wanted: every day if he was up to it. I also told them that I thought it would be better for everyone, them included, to be near home, nearer to town and people and help. It was going to be a difficult time, and it was important to be together. They didn't have any idea just how hard it was going to get, and I wasn't even sure myself. I only knew it wasn't going to be easy. I don't think the girls knew to even think about it at this point.

They went to bed that night emotionally exhausted and slept twelve hours or more. Kurt got up relatively early but wasn't feeling well at all. The pain in his abdomen was severe. He slept on the couch and had a fever. At one point, he sat up, curling up tightly to try to alleviate some of the pain. He looked up at me and said, "I really don't want to be here anymore like this." I knew he was telling me the truth.

Later that morning, the pain had subsided somewhat, and we were able to talk before the girls got up. "Kurt, would you consider coming to our house in town? I think it might be helpful to you and important for the girls' sake as well."

"Oh, I never wanted you to have to be a caregiver again, Shawn."

I was touched that he would have even thought about that. But I told him that I didn't mind at all, that I wanted him to come and be with us. He said right away, "Well, I would like to be in town . . . I have a lot of people I know who would come by to see me, and I know it would be best for the girls." It was settled.

Hospice came for the first time early that next week. Following the initial visit to complete all the paperwork, a wonderful male nurse came to see Kurt. When I first opened the door with the sun gleaming in as he entered our foyer, I noticed something odd about his skin and wondered if he had cancer himself. As we began to talk, this genuinely inquisitive man earnestly wanted to know all about Kurt, how he was feeling physically and began to ask a number of questions, one right after the other.

"Are there things you want to accomplish right now, Kurt? Are you worried or afraid? Do you feel comfortable where you're at? Do you feel loved?"

Right here, Kurt answered with an emphatic, unhesitating *"Yes!"*

After four or five more questions, the nurse for some reason asked Kurt this question again. "Kurt, do you feel loved?"

Again, as emphatic as the first time, Kurt responded, *"Yes, yes, I do."*

I knew his answer was significant. He had crossed a line in his mind. Yes, he did know that we all loved him, his girls all loved him. All the years of him feeling lowly, unloved, and even hating himself seemed to have melted away. This was the only question the nurse asked him twice. His answer was significant. A battle in his heart and mind had been won. And for me, there was healing in his words.

As the nurse talked and typed, I noticed that he was missing several fingers; then I noticed in the sunlight that part of one ear was gone. He had been burned. As he stayed longer, he mentioned that God would see Kurt through this, and then his own story emerged.

He had been in an auto accident in our valley many years before when he was a senior in high school. Interestingly, his accident was only about a half mile from where Kurt's had been. We had a wonderful talk. Now all these years following his accident, he was still serving people in his profession with such great care and compassion. *Amazing what God will do with a surrendered life,* I thought. God had sent an angel that day to show me the healing that had been done in Kurt's heart, and I was thankful.

Over the next days, the girls faithfully did all they could do to help their dad: get his meds, make him protein smoothies in between meals of soft foods, soups, yogurt, etc. They talked and snuggled and laughed at Dad's funny jokes. Emma and Rebecca drove him out to his home quite a few times in the first ten days, helping him to do the things he wanted to accomplish.

He worked on paying bills and doing an inventory of his shop equipment and tools. He taught Emma how to use an engraver. Then he gave the girls the last, special gift he would give them: toolboxes, treasure boxes really, with their names engraved on them and filled with his treasured, well-worn tools. He had loved his craft. Over the years, he truly had become a master craftsman. Now he was giving his treasured possessions to his three precious girls. He didn't have diamonds to give them, but his tools were worth more than gold or diamonds now to the girls.

Somehow when the end nears, what matters changes—it changes a lot. Sitting together for hours, even enjoying a nap at the same time, or a hug, all seem more important than any vacation you'll ever take. Though these moments were hard, I know none of us would have traded them for anything.

Kurt and I had talks we hadn't really planned on having again. Although I hadn't wanted to be the trustee on his trust when we divorced, I was glad now that he had insisted on me being the only one he trusted to take care of our girls and their best interests. All his affairs—work, personal, financial—had to be put in order, and we both sensed it needed to be done now. Although I was working in Reno as an accountant for a private trust company, I was able to reduce my hours. Mid-summer I gave my employer a six-month notice to resign, as I somehow knew that I would be Kurt's primary caregiver. I wouldn't want to continue to commute such a distance; I'd figure something out for work closer to home and be nearer to help Kurt.

Our girls would all be leaving within a couple of weeks for Southern California for college and for work. Allie had graduated from college, and it was hard to believe that our youngest would be a freshman and Emma a junior. The girls talked about college: should they go, or stay home and be with their dad for as long as he is here? They both were very willing to stay. They would perhaps risk losing their academic scholarships if they didn't go back, but that was not their most primary concern.

In the end, Kurt and I felt they were to continue with their plans. God had provided for them to be in school at this time, and we encouraged them to stay the course. We just needed to trust that He would show us differently if they were to change their plans.

At first, Kurt insisted on sleeping on the couch. But after a few days, it was obvious that he really needed the comfort of a bed, and I had him take my room, which was downstairs and had its own bathroom. He seemed to get more unstable on his feet at times, especially at moments when the pain caused his whole body to shake, sometimes uncontrollably. Although he was in more and more pain, he didn't complain. We increased his meds as he seemed to need it, but each day he would get up relatively early and shower, get dressed and come out into the living room for the day to begin.

Many people came by to visit Kurt during the days. About two weeks after Kurt came to the house, the hospice chaplain called and made an appointment to come see Kurt the next day. When I got home from work, Nate, a long-time friend, was there visiting. After he left, Kurt seemed tired but made a point of telling me that he had a wonderful visit with the chaplain, Dan. They visited for a long time and prayed together. Kurt was glad that he had come. I was happy for him.

It wasn't until later that I learned more about their visit.

Other people came by, and once again our home was a place of people pouring out their love for Kurt. My brother and his wife, family, friends, his and mine, and ours came by, all eager to visit with Kurt. One evening when I got home from work, Kurt's attorney had come to visit him. It was the first time I had ever met him after all these years. When he was ready to leave, I walked him to the door. He paused on the threshold. He didn't seem to want to move, or perhaps he couldn't. I realized that tears were streaming down his face. He couldn't talk.

I could feel his pain. We stood there together for a long time. Words didn't seem needed. They wouldn't have been adequate, anyway. Finally, I hugged him and thanked him for coming.

Many others came: some who had turned away from me; others who had loved us both through the years. Our lives had collided again, and so had the people from our separate circles.

Jeannie called one afternoon wanting to come to see Kurt with her husband, Greg. She had been in the hospital herself recently and was recovering with Guillain-Barre, a rare disorder in which the immune system attacks the nerves of the body. I told her that she didn't need to do that, that it was important for her not to over-exert or stress herself; she needed rest to eventually recover from this serious illness. But, true to Jeannie-style, she insisted that she was coming over to see Kurt, to see us. She had to come.

As she came into the living room where Kurt was sitting, she immediately sank down on the floor, kneeling in front of Kurt. Greg stood behind her. "Kurt, all these years you've told people how you always wanted to get your girls back, to have your family back. Well, you never probably thought it would happen in this way. God has given you what you've wanted, Kurt. It has happened."

Through tears, she paused, trying to get her composure. "This is the greatest story of restoration and redemption that I have ever seen," she said. She was holding his hand. Kurt was nodding. Tears streamed down all of our faces. Yes, she had traveled through the years, each and every one, with us—she was seeing the end of the story, too. Bitter but sweet. His story, our story. Once again, time stood still.

That next Saturday morning, we had prepared for Kurt's uncle and two cousins to come from the Bay Area. Early that morning I heard the shower running like usual—Kurt was up, getting ready to meet with his family. After a while, I no longer heard the shower running, and Kurt still had not come out.

"Kurt?" I called. When he didn't respond, I came through the door and found him slumped down on my bed with a towel draped over him. Startled, I shook him and called his name, "Kurt! Please, Kurt!"

He didn't respond at first. Then he started to move and sat up slowly, clumsily, slumping forward. He didn't say a word, but he had his socks in his hand and was acting like he wanted to put them on.

"Do you want to get dressed, Kurt?" Yes, he did. I helped him dress. Then he looked up at me and said clearly, "I think that was my last unassisted shower." *Yes, maybe,* I thought to myself.

Suddenly, that day, it seemed like things had shifted. He was obviously declining. Emma helped me get Kurt to the couch, but instead of visiting, wanting his drink and meds, he laid down on the couch to sleep. When his uncle and cousins arrived, he sat up and tried with all his might to visit. I could see the immense effort he was putting out to try to hold a conversation. He would answer a question and then get off track on something that didn't even make sense, his thoughts and words wandering. I know the girls were uncomfortable, as I'm sure his cousins and uncle were too, but they didn't show it.

When Kurt had to go to the restroom, Emma and I came each on one side of his tall, thin body, got underneath his shoulders, and helped him shuffle his way to the restroom. I had flashes of his head injury and those many months of life after his accident. Seemed like we were back at that same place, in a strange way, and so suddenly.

We helped him return to the living room to visit. He had so looked forward to his family coming, but it was all he could do to sit upright. They stayed just long enough but seemed to recognize that Kurt needed to be able to rest and not be stressed, and graciously left before much time had passed. My head was spinning.

Was it the toxins? What was causing him to suddenly act so differently, so compromised? *Perhaps the rest and a quiet afternoon will help him return to normal,* I thought.

It didn't.

Chapter 17

Eternal Moments

That day seemed so long. We were all struggling to process the change. Kurt slept most of the day, trying to "come out of it," to eat and then to visit. It was difficult for him, difficult for us. Allie was coming back on Wednesday, now just four days away. It was important for her to get home.

Emma and I had been camping out near the door of Kurt's room for the past couple of nights, wanting to be near if Kurt got up to use the restroom or needed help. That night I could see the exhaustion on both Emmie's and Becky's faces, and I encouraged Emma to go upstairs to their bedroom to get some sleep. She so wanted to be helpful, to be there to help. I assured her I would call her and Rebecca if I needed them.

It was sometime around midnight. For some reason I was still up, putting some dishes away when I heard the toilet flush in my bathroom. I quickly went into the bedroom to see Kurt shuffling slowly, hanging on to the wall and then the chair. Before I could say a word, he looked me straight in the eyes and said, "What has happened to me today? Have I had a stroke or something? I don't even have my land legs!"

Without a pause, I said to him, "I don't know, Kurt. But I think that the Lord is going to take you home soon." The words didn't seem mine. As he gazed back at me, there was a look in his eyes of surprise, but also of instant acceptance of a new reality. He didn't say a word. I helped shuffle him back to bed and tucked him in. We prayed. I laid on the floor keeping watch.

The next morning, I was up early, and again I heard the water running and keep on running. Entering the bathroom, I saw Kurt sitting on the toilet seat next to the tub, trying to get his lower legs over into the tub without success. Again, my heart and head went back to those months following Kurt's head injury. *Déjà vu*, certainly. His clumsy legs would not cooperate with his head.

"Kurt, would you like to take a shower?"

He only nodded. After more than fifty years of showering daily, it was just the very first thing he was going to do, even today. I helped him slip into the tub and wash his body using the hand-held showerhead. Somehow, we got his tall, frail frame out of the tub, and I once again helped him dress. Yes, yesterday had been his last unassisted shower.

It was Sunday, and the four of us just stayed in. The day seemed long; Kurt again slept more and only wanted liquids. By mid-afternoon, I knew I would need to call hospice tomorrow morning to ask for a shower chair and a hospital bed. Kurt was now having difficulty making it to the restroom. By evening, I was struggling with the thought of asking for a catheter. Somehow, deep down inside, having that thought meant the end was near. How could this be? Things seemed to be happening so fast.

At 5:30 the next morning, I called hospice and left a message. They called back: yes, we needed a bed, a catheter, probably no shower chair.

That morning our nurse friend Carllene showed up. I was so glad to see her. She just always seemed to be there on those days when I really needed her. She visited with the girls and a little with Kurt. Hospice was bringing the medical bed by mid-day, but we would have to wait for the paramedics who would come to transfer Kurt into the bed.

As we waited, Kurt and I laid down together on the bed. And once again, he said those words I had heard so many times before, but only with a gentleness now: "I don't want to belabor it, but it nearly killed me when you left with the girls."

For the first time, I responded: "I believe you, Kurt. I totally understand what you are saying and how you felt. I get it. But the truth is . . . it nearly killed *me* to stay as long as I did. And I too felt like I died when I left. But I didn't do it to hurt you. I did it for the sake of our girls, for their well-being and protection, and to give them some sense of normal."

He was quiet for a moment. "I know that now," he said at last. Pausing again, he said, "I really can't explain it all, what happened . . . I just went crazy."

It felt as if the circle had closed. This was an answer to a crazy world—our world. At least in part. The years seemed to collapse now into this one moment. Somehow, to me, it all seemed to make sense.

As difficult as it was, Emma and Rebecca continued to come in to spend time with their dad. Would he be here to see them off to their next year at school, with orientation just a week away? Should they go; should they stay? I know their minds must have been racing as their young hearts were breaking. They needed their dad. They needed him, and now time was robbing them. Time was closing in on all of us. I felt it. I know they must have felt it, too.

Kurt was becoming less lucid. Around noon, he was sitting up with his back against the headboard of the bed. Carllene was in the room with me when Kurt said with his eyes closed, "I'm getting closer and closer to the spiritual."

Surprised by his words, I said to him, "Well, Kurt, have you seen Jesus yet?"

"No, not yet." He paused. "I have a lot to teach Him." Pausing again, "He has a lot to teach me."

I knew in my heart that things were right with Kurt and God. Jesus had the final say in his life: He was the One on the throne.

As we continued to wait for the bed and the paramedics, Stacey, Kurt's previous girlfriend, came by to see him. She had called to see if she could come by. I had agreed, feeling it was important to her, and probably to him, too. Somehow I was glad that she could see him one last time. Funny, but I felt an ache in my heart for her.

Finally, the paramedics came around two that afternoon. The big, strapping young men reminded me of those who had come to our door that Friday night in November of 1993—only now they seemed so young. For some reason this time, I couldn't watch them transfer him into the bed.

That night both Emma and I stayed in my bed so that we could be there to hear Kurt if he needed us. I wished that Em didn't have to be there, waiting and keeping watch with me, but I was thankful for the comfort of her presence. I know I didn't sleep much. She probably didn't, either. Rebecca stayed on the couch, near but not too close.

Early the next morning we got our mugs of coffee and gathered around Kurt. Emmie and Becky were there, both brave as their hearts could allow. I read something out of the book of Psalms, hoping it would bring us comfort. We prayed, Kurt, agreeing and saying Amen, squeezing our hands and responding when we would tell him that we loved him.

"We love you, Dad . . . We love you like crazy."

"I love you, too."

It seemed to say it all. Nothing else seemed to matter. Nothing at all.

Allie had decided to return to Santa Barbara for work the week before, saying she needed to be there. In the restaurant business, weekends are certainly the busiest times, but I think that was her way of coping. I tried to talk to her about the decision, saying that she didn't want to have any regrets, that time was maybe short. She had cried really hard one night before leaving, but her decision remained the same. I think she too had to put some distance between her heart and the situation.

On Tuesday, Kurt's responses were quickly lessening, his words fewer. I called hospice as I sensed time drawing near, closing in on us. His breathing was heavy and rattling. Hospice seemed reluctant to send the nurse out, but I was feeling a little uneasy, not knowing for sure what was happening or what else we should be doing. I just needed someone to tell me something, to give us more direction. Kurt was on his way out, and I didn't quite know what to do.

We continued to administer the pain medication. Emma stayed in the room with me much of the day. Rebecca came in to pray in the morning but spent much of the day on the couch. It seemed she too had to put some space between her and the death of her dad. She seemed numb. Of course, she was; this was her daddy. One day a seemingly healthy man, capable and hard-working, still making funny jokes, making her laugh, making us all laugh in Kurt's signature way. Within a few short days, he was reduced to someone thinner, more frail, and in some ways unrecognizable as the strapping, strong dad she knew and loved. It seemed surreal to me. I know it must have to her, and to Emma, too.

But amazingly, in those last hours, Kurt seemed to become even more handsome to us. I mentioned to the girls what Dad had shared with me in one of the very first letters he wrote to me: that some people thought he looked like Robert Redford. We laughed at his candid joke, even way back then. But now Emmie said, "Oh, I can see that."

Finally, the nurse came by briefly to see Kurt. She didn't stay long, tried to tell me that this was "normal." *Normal*—what's that? How many times had I seen someone pass from this life on to the next? I didn't know this was normal. She did say it would probably be sometime next week, maybe longer. *What? Longer than a week?* I felt in my heart that wasn't true. I know that's why hospice hesitated to send the nurse; they thought that he had more time. He didn't. I knew that.

Karen and her husband Craig (an ER doctor) stopped by to check on Kurt, and on us on their way out of town for their anniversary. When they left, Craig indicated it probably wouldn't be too long, confirming what I knew in my heart. Karen and her mom and sisters had walked this journey of life together with us for twenty years. It seemed right and good to have them here with us, even briefly. There don't have to be many words at times like these. In fact, often fewer words are far more comforting than many. I was grateful for their coming.

Emma was so courageous, staying in the room most of the day, giving Kurt his meds, helping me change the sheets, wiping his face with a washcloth. It seemed so wrong to see our daughter, so young, barely out of teenage years, ministering the last acts of love to her dad as he was so obviously slipping away from us. Oh, how I wanted to take the pain away for her. I was her mom; that was my job, wasn't it? But I couldn't just make it go away this time. Time, eternity, it seemed, was at the door. There was no way to turn it back now, to refuse it. He comes when He is ready.

On Tuesday late afternoon, I was standing by Kurt's bed, and his head was turned slightly toward the open window. The bit of rain and wind blew some freshness into the room. Kurt hadn't said anything since early morning. Then he turned toward me with his chin raised and his lips puckered as if to be kissed. I kissed his thin lips lightly.

He opened his eyes and said, "From now on, when I see you, that's what I want from you: to be bonded to you. It's important to me." Tears welled in my eyes. He closed his eyes and puckered his lips again. I kissed him gently one last time.

He opened his eyes and said again, "This is what I want from you. It's important to me."

"It's important to me too, Kurt." I swallowed hard to keep the tears from pouring out, but still, they escaped.

Tuesday night, I knew we were all exhausted. It is hard work to let go. It's painful to say goodbye when those are words you don't want to say, ever. I think we know deep down inside we are meant *not* to say goodbye. There is a sense of permanence, of eternity, and we don't want to let go. I told Emma that I would stay in my room that night with Kurt, that it was important for her to get some sleep. I stayed with Kurt, hearing his breathing get more shallow. I dozed on and off, never really sleeping.

Sometime after midnight, I went to the restroom and getting a fresh towel out of the linen closet, I noticed a stack of special cards and letters at the back of the cabinet. Among these were two birthday "gifts," letters I had written to Kurt early in our relationship. The first one I had given to him for his thirty-fourth birthday, while we were just dating, and I had titled it, *God and You and Me—An Introduction.* The second "gift" was given to him six years later, on his fortieth birthday.

I grabbed a blanket and snuggled into the chair next to Kurt's bed and began to read the first birthday gift. I had shared excerpts from our initial letters and conversations, the importance of our families, work, the things we loved to do. I shared my faith as a Christian. Kurt's response: *I see God's presence in the sparkling eyes of a laughing child, in a mountain meadow full of wild flowers, or a flock of geese in a chilly December sky . . .* I couldn't help but think that he, too, loved to write and had a such a way with words on paper, and a sensitivity to things.

The "gift" reflected our talks about my mom, my possible move to the area, Kurt's business, his need for a business partner to "run the business side of things."

I chronicled our first dates, our discussions about God, our hopes and dreams for our lives. He told me that he felt God had been chasing him for some time. I had given him a Bible in those first months of dating, with the following inscription: "My heart for you, Kurt, is summed up in the following verses, *'I have not stopped giving thanks for you, remembering you in my prayers. I keep asking that the God of our Lord Jesus Christ, the glorious Father, may give you the Spirit of wisdom and revelation, so that you may know him better . . .'"* (Ephesians 1:16-17, NIV).

The gift ended with the first *I love you* spoken. "I'm crazy about you, you know. Unequivocally crazy about you." "I know, me too." Our meeting one another was summed up in these words:

An introduction, I think so. A beginning, perhaps.
A miracle, for sure.

As I wiped the tears from my eyes, I didn't know if I could read on. Opening the second letter, I was plunged back in time in our marriage when we already had Allie, who would turn three the next day. Emma was just fifteen months old, and I had just found out I was pregnant again. This was eight months before Rebecca was born; nine months before Kurt's accident.

This birthday gift was addressed to "My dearest Kurt on your fortieth birthday—"

An introduction, indeed. A beginning, for sure.
A miracle, no doubt.

Six years ago today I helped you celebrate your thirty-fourth birthday, the first of many that I would be privileged to share with you as my husband. At the time, February 6, 1987, I didn't consciously think I'd be spending a lifetime of birthdays with you. But as I read the birthday gift I gave to you on that special day, *God and You and Me—An Introduction*, I realize now that my heart must have known that God was at work beginning to weave together a tapestry that would take our lifetimes to complete.

As with any tapestry, you can't really discern the picture, the story depicted on the front by looking at the tapestry's back—it's just a jumbled-looking mess of threads. It's only when you turn it over and gaze at the front that the maze of threads artfully woven together makes sense, and the artist's intent and story can be clearly seen and fully understood.

I must admit that I have made the mistake of looking at "our tapestry" from the backside, sometimes seeing only a mess of thread seemingly without direction or purpose, loose ends here and there, and   . . . no clear picture, no real story. But as I read this record dated February 6, 1987, of our meeting, our correspondence, and talks, our thoughts and questions and prayers, I amazingly find that I am no longer looking at the backside of our tapestry but at the front.

A picture, clear and focused.
A plan. A purpose. And, yes, a story.
A love story without question . . . Undeniable.

God's plan. Our lives. His will. Our walk.

Yes, I see it, oh, so clearly now . . . His hand. Our lives. Masterfully, artfully woven together. God and You and Me . . . But wait, the picture is evolving—not by chance, but by the touch of the Master's Hand:

God
    and You . . .
        and Me . . .
            and Allie . . .
                and Emma . . .
                    and . . .

His will. Our lives.

An introduction. A beginning. No end.

A miracle. Yes, a miracle, indeed.

Wiping the tears streaming from my eyes, I realized now that our tapestry, our story, had begun over twenty years ago. My life intertwined with Kurt's from the beginning to the end. Though the story sat in a box nearly forgotten, almost thrown away, life was not over for us quite yet. His story, my story, our story—with its final chapter still to be written. Tears were my companion that night, but they were accompanied by a soft sense of wonder in a God who knows all things, from the beginning to the end, the Master Weaver of each of our lives, who never gives up, who never lets us go. His story—ours. Ours—His.

When the girls got up the next morning, they immediately came into the bedroom. We all three prayed again with and for Kurt, but he no longer responded or acknowledged our prayers or our presence. It was hard to stay but even harder to leave. I couldn't believe we were at this place. It didn't seem like all that many years ago that I was by Kurt's bedside when he was in a coma for those many weeks, and our girls were just babies. Now, they were young women, and here we all were at his bedside again, after all these years. Life had passed us by in some ways. And now, too soon, it was time to say goodbye.

Kurt had not said a word all morning. Early afternoon, as I was standing by his bed, he turned to me suddenly with eyes opened wide. "I'm really going to miss you!"

"I'm really going to miss you too, Kurt." This time, the tears just overflowed. The pain of many years seemed to flood my whole being, surpassed only by the knowledge that time would soon be no more—for Kurt, for us, for our girls—as a family.

Those were his very last spoken words.

He passed away about six hours later. I knew in my heart—he had gone home.

Part Five
Restoration

— Chapter 18 —

A Woman's Heart

We long for something permanent: something lasting that we can count on. Often we look for it in our marriages, and so we should. Marriage was meant to be permanent. It is a covenant to be kept for a lifetime. Yet women and men . . . we fail one another. Our marriages are as human as we are. We hunger for constancy and permanence, and while it is a beautiful thing to have a marriage that lasts, even those in happy marriages will tell you: we cannot fulfill our need for constancy there. We must send our roots down deeper, down into the heart of God, who is our eternal and constant home.

Sometimes our earthly marriages reflect the constancy of God: *What God has joined together, let no man separate.* Sometimes our marriages disintegrate, and we mourn. To all of us, the happily married, the divorced, those in troubled marriages, the call of God is the same: we must make our home in Him, in the only true Faithful One, the initiator and keeper of the covenant (Jeremiah 31:33-34). He has loved us, forever, with an everlasting love. He gives us a new heart toward Him—a heart to love Him—and then He writes His law upon our hearts and minds, causing us, through the power of His Holy Spirit, to walk with Him.

And when we fail and fall (and we all do at times), we know that we have One who intercedes for us before the Father. One who has already paid the price for the forgiveness of our sins (all of them: past, present, and future), and we are forgiven, seen as righteous in God's sight. It is His keeping power that holds us in right relationship with Him. He sanctifies His bride. He has done it all.

And oh, how we need Him to do it.

For many of us women, we want to know that we are of such great worth, great value, that our men would be so chivalrous as to lay down their lives for us. We want to be treasured, kept, valued. We have a King who made us, created us, this way. It is right, and it is good.

When we look around us in our culture, it is easy to believe that men are different: that they don't have needs like we do, to be precious and valued. We imagine that they are invulnerable in ways we are not. We think men do not have tender hearts like we do, and that they have affairs, use pornography, and relate to sexuality in a more callused manner, untouched and unfeeling. Unaffected. We feel exposed and vulnerable, at the mercy of our husbands, waiting for the inevitable infidelity, the broken covenant that seems almost a guarantee. Most of us went into our marriages with divorce statistics hovering over our hearts like a thundercloud. Instead of feeling like the princesses God intended us to be—the only one our husbands have eyes for—we often feel like a ragged old doll, worn out by an unseen battle.

But God, our gracious, compassionate, covenant-keeping God, does not see us that way, despite how we feel. We are each His bride and part of the Bride of Christ: treasured, cherished and bound to Him through a covenant initiated and kept by God Himself. One that cannot be broken or torn apart. He is a covenant-keeping God who cannot be other than true to His promises.

Our fears and false beliefs would steal our joy and our sense of safety in marriage. It is hard to unlearn these ways of thinking and allow God to slowly transform our minds and hearts, to let His perfect love cast out all our fears. Yet He is our faithful, heavenly husband—our King, whose patience and tender care will never leave us. He does not grow weary of helping us, and He will be with us until the end.

In our marriages, there is better to be had. We do not need to live beneath the lies and the fears. We were made for so much more. We do not need to accept what we have been told: men are from Mars and women from Venus, so we'll never understand each other or be understood. The truth is—men and women are both from Earth. We are God's children, far more alike than we are different. And there is great hope in that truth.

For men, they are taught from an early age not to show emotion. *That's girl stuff, sissy stuff*, they learn. That lie does lifelong damage. Men, just like women, are emotional creatures; they, too, need access to both tenderness and toughness, to being cherished and to cherish. But as young boys, they soon see that they will be mocked or punished for showing "weakness." So they hide it beneath a mask of invulnerability, pretending they're unaffected when they are just as touched by pain and joy as women are. The only emotion left that they're allowed to show is anger—which often destroys the very intimacy they (like all of us) so desperately need.

This isolation is only compounded by the way our society and the Church handles the issue of pornography and sexuality. Though we say with our mouths that "sin is sin," with our actions we are telling a different story. Some sins can be spoken of publicly, confessed without the threat of condemnation or ostracism. Others—like sexual sins? Those we treat as unspeakable, monstrous. And who but a monster would do something monstrous—right? *Maybe that's just what I am, at my core,* men begin to believe. *Maybe I'm just a monster. A scumbag. No good.* Unsurprisingly, someone who believes they're nothing but a monster usually behaves like one, which confirms their belief that they're nothing but a monster, incapable of living differently. It's a vicious cycle.

We create a perfect environment for shame to thrive when we make sexuality something fraught with taboo, silence, and scary religious judgment. Dr. Brené Brown teaches that the best antidote to shame is *empathy*: to hear "Me too." To be seen, without judgment. To know we're not the only ones, and we're not a lost cause. We are worthy of love and belonging because we were made by One who loves us, One to whom we eternally belong.

Imagine how different the outcome would be, for men and women both, if we could speak of sexual struggles and encourage one another just as though we were speaking of an addiction to fast food or the struggle to incorporate regular exercise into our lives?

Social science is increasingly showing us that pornography damages the quality of our intimate relationships—but so, we are learning, does too much time spent on our iPhones. People addicted to pornography aren't more morally monstrous than people who have developed an addiction to scrolling through social media. They're not "beyond the pale" of human community; they're right here with the rest of us, and our struggles are the same.

It is in this light of radical acceptance and belonging that we are able to open ourselves to God's transformation. Men and women with shame around their sexuality come to know they are not monsters, fatally flawed, disgusting, and unworthy of love and belonging. They would know they are just the same as all of us. They are not alone. In fact, they are in good company. And because of that, they can shake themselves free—with the help of God and of loving community—from things that damage them and people around them, and that get in the way of the joyful intimacy they crave. In this spirit of compassion and acceptance, men and women can help one another tackle the urgency of sexual addiction in our culture, breaking the silence, dispelling the shame, and taking responsibility together for cultivating the love and constancy we long for in our marriages—the love and constancy God designed for us to have—the love and constancy that mirror Christ's love for the Church.

No matter how ragged we may be or feel, or how long we have felt face-down in the mud, or how many times we have been walked on, or our backs nearly broken, we have One, the One Who Knows All Things, who says "Come, look up, my beautiful bride. You, yes, you. I am the lifter of your head. Arise and walk securely with Me, your Groom and Great Lover."

It is this God who knows all things, who knows your bride-like longing heart, who lifts your head and who has your back. With Him, there is no disgrace. Just love and grace and goodness. He, Jesus, is Faithful and True. He will never disappoint or fail or reject you. Ever.

— Chapter 19 —

The Rainbow ... The Promise

Within minutes of Kurt's passing, Jeannie called just to check in. Amazingly, miraculously, she was there with us again, having traveled this journey from beginning to end.

We somehow got through the next couple of days. Thankfully, I had gone to the funeral home to make the final arrangements days earlier. My friend Gloria had been kind enough to go with me. Now I was glad that part was over, and we could just be home. There were lots of calls and other arrangements and the need for the girls and me just to be together.

Emma and Allie had to return to Southern California on Saturday night following Kurt's passing, as Em had to start her job on campus as an orientation leader. Rebecca would need to leave for her freshman orientation at Westmont on Tuesday. We hadn't even planned or prepared for the start of school. It seemed like we were lost in another world, not conscious of the mundane, the "life issues." We had been trying to hang on and help Kurt. Now he was gone, and we were trying to wrestle with reality. We decided that Kurt's memorial service would be held in two weeks so the girls could have their first weeks trying somehow to get through orientation and the start of school. We planned to shop for Rebecca's dorm room on Saturday.

That morning I woke up early, around 6:15 or so, and quietly made my way into the sunroom. It's my favorite spot in our house, framed with huge windows overlooking green ranchland with the Sierras jetting majestically up in the distance. I had not been alone or had quiet time for what seemed like a long time. It was just light outside, and it had continued to drizzle rain on and off, as it had all week.

As I sat down, I sunk into my own body, feeling heavy, wanting to cry. I felt prompted, though, to look up. As I looked out into the field of green, the pastureland behind our house, dawn just presenting itself, I saw this beautiful rainbow with a stream of light shining directly into the field. It seemed so near, literally in our backyard.

Looking at it, I remembered: In the Bible, the rainbow is a symbol of a promise.

Immediately, I heard those familiar words: *"Did I not tell you that if you believe, you will see the glory of God?"* Tears streamed down my face. I knew the Lord was saying, "Kurt is home, he is home, with Me." I sat there for what seemed a long time. All was quiet.

I so wanted to capture this rainbow on camera, to memorialize this moment. But my cell phone wasn't charged, and my camera had a dead battery. At barely 6:30 a.m., I didn't want to wake the girls to find their phones. So I sat back down in my chair to drink in the glory of this moment and to watch the rainbow until it disappeared.

In that time, I had a keen sense of God's very nearness to me. I once again opened my Bible and re-

read John 11, the word given to me nearly twenty years earlier.

Emmanuel. Emmanuel, God with us. Yes, I had, we had, indeed seen His glory.

On that following Monday morning, as Becky and I were loading the Yukon with her things for college, my cell phone rang. It was the hospice chaplain, Dan. "Shawn, not sure if you know me, but I came to see Kurt a little more than a week ago." Yes, I told him, I knew he had visited.

Dan was calling with condolences from the hospice staff. "We cannot believe that God took Kurt home so quickly. None of us could believe it. He was doing so well when I saw him just ten days ago. We are all so sorry for your loss."

He went on to tell me how Allie was there, having invited him in, and how Kurt had talked about his three wonderful girls and how very proud he was of them. "What I feel compelled to tell you," Dan continued, "is that Kurt shared how you were instrumental in drawing him back to the Lord. He talked a lot about these past few months and how being able to be with you, praying together again . . ."

He paused, but the lump in my throat wouldn't let me talk. He went on: "Kurt knew he was loved by you and your girls. He certainly told me that he had done a lot of wrong things in his life, made many bad choices. But I told him, 'Oh, but haven't we all, Kurt? Isn't that what *grace* is all about?'"

"'Yes,' Kurt said to me, nodding. 'Yes, that is what *grace* is all about.'"

Dan shared that they had spoken of Christ's own worthiness in our place—that it is He who makes us worthy. The chaplain went on to tell me that he had rarely seen such peace in someone in Kurt's circumstances. He even said to Kurt at one point, "But isn't it a bummer, Kurt, all that you're going through?"

Kurt looked up directly at him and, spanning the room with his arm, said, "Oh, but look where I am!" I knew something to be certain: Kurt knew he was so very loved, and in his world, his life, and now for all eternity, he was at last truly and perfectly at peace.

— Chapter 20 —

Bowing Down: The Dance of Grace

The God Chasers. Or is it: *God* the Chaser?

I think it is the latter. We simply cannot chase God until He has first chased us.

Sounds familiar. It is not that we first loved Him, but that He first loved us (1 John 4:10). God is the chaser. *The* Chaser. We are the pursued.

We, the first loved. He, the lover. Him first. All else follows. We run, and we even sometimes hide. But God, the Eternal Chaser, does not give up easily. In fact, He never gives up. He's God. He loves us with an eternal love, an everlasting love. He is the Everlasting Father. Not like ones, we may have known here on earth, but as our heavenly Father, loving us with a love that is unending, eternal, a love that *never says never*.

As the good Shepherd followed that lost and fearful lamb into the wilderness where it had become stranded, so the Lover of our soul, the Giver of our life, the One who has called us by name, will search for us and find us and carry us safely home. In your own wilderness wandering, keep listening for His voice; the Lord of lords and the King of kings is calling for you. Do you hear Him? Will you answer?

I believe that God is serious about our salvation. How silly to say. He sent His only Son, His only Begotten Son, Jesus Christ, to this earth—God

Incarnate, full of grace and truth—to live and die and be resurrected from the dead just to pay the penalty for our sins. Each of our sins. We the guilty, me the guilty. Him, the Innocent. Sounds crazy, but it's true.

Why in the world would He do such a thing? "For God so loved the world that He gave His One and Only Son that whosoever would believe in Him shall not perish but have eternal life." Period. That's it. That is the good news of the Gospel. God loves us so much that He died in our place through the offering of a perfect sacrifice. Crazy? Yes, absolutely. He's God. It's His plan, His will. His offering. Our hope.

I believe too that God takes us seriously when He offers us salvation and we accept, we believe however weakly, even a bit less than wholeheartedly. Being God the Chaser, He is in pursuit of the ones He loves. A plan from the beginning: it cost Him everything, His own life through His Son, and He will chase and find us.

For Kurt, I believe that he accepted Christ and believed in Him for his salvation while we were dating. I also believe that he thought that in coming to Christ, his old habits, and even addictions, might just be taken away, his problems solved as a Christian. But it's not that simple. Old habits, really "old natures," die hard.

I look back on Kurt's life and mourn. I mourn all the pain he suffered and the pain he caused. I mourn for all the things we didn't know: about brain injury, about the connection between shame and addiction, about ourselves, about each other. I mourn for the marriage we could have had—the marriage that was broken by trauma, by deceit, by abuse and betrayal. I mourn for what our girls lost—for what Kurt lost—for what I lost. And in that mourning, my faithful Comforter holds my hand and speaks words of peace and new life into my heart. Those final days—twenty, to be exact—with Kurt at home: I am grateful for the closeness we shared then, he and I together, all of us together once again as a family.

And I look back on Kurt's life—on our lives—and rejoice too, somehow. For a time, it seemed that the darkness had won. But the light shines in the darkness, and the darkness cannot overcome it. Our God, the Chaser, followed us into the wilderness, and He spoke tenderly to us, and He healed our wounds. He never gives up. We despair and cannot see the way forward; all around us seems like darkest night; we think we have lost ourselves forever. But He finds us, no matter how hidden, how hopeless, how lost. Thank God—He finds us.

The road to new life is a long one, and thank goodness, we have a patient and loving Father and Helper, the Great Lover of our soul who wants to lead, to guide us every step of the way. As our hearts are humbled, we can see dimly, as through a veil for now— but we can see.

Bowing down is not really bowing down until it comes from the heart. We cannot bow until it is within us, until our heart has yielded. It is like a dance. There is One who leads, and the true partner must follow. But the pursued partner must want to dance.

The Lead is a gentleman. He will not force, but He does pursue. The Chaser may coax and corner. He may prod and herd. He may shout through our situations and circumstances. He may just whisper and wait.

He has time. In fact, He holds it in his hands. He is patient. He is kind, slow to anger and abounding in love, great love. And He is faithful. Faithful to keep calling, beckoning us to the dance floor. He waits. He waits until we are willing—and not just willing, but wanting. The dance of grace takes two, in the giving and the receiving of this great gift: Grace.

The perfect, holy, righteous, all-loving God waits for us to take His hand of grace, and He gently leads us to the floor, to the stage of life where the dance begins. He, the lead. We, the partner. He, the pursuer. We, the pursued.

When we finally get it, we can bow low before the Giver of all life and all that is good. We can finally see clearly this One who has been calling our name, beckoning us to a dance that we have waited for all our lives. We can, at last, reach up and take the Hand that has been extended to us our whole life. We just didn't see . . . until now.

Now we behold Him, the One who has called us from eternity past. He is the Ancient of Days, the great I AM, the Alpha and the Omega, the Beginning and the End. Though He holds the sun and the moon in their places, He still has hands ever reaching out toward us, beckoning us to come. "Come, dance with me," the Great Lover of our soul whispers. He gives what we don't deserve. When we finally see, we receive it gladly, gratefully.

Sometime during the summer, Kurt reached up to take hold of the hand, the One who had been calling his name and bowed low. When the chaplain from hospice came to see him, it was apparent then that Kurt knew.

Grace. Isn't that what it's all about?

~~~~~~~~~~~~~~~~~~~~~~~

For this reason
I bow my knees before the Father,
from whom every family in heaven
and on earth derives its name,
that He would grant you,
according to the riches of His glory,
to be strengthened with power
through His Spirit in the inner man,
so that Christ may dwell in your
hearts through faith;
and that you, being rooted and grounded in
love,
may be able to comprehend
with all the saints
what is the breadth and length
and height and depth,
and to know the love of Christ
which surpasses knowledge,
that you may be filled up
to all the fullness of God.
~ Ephesians 3:14-19

~~~~~~~~~~~~~~~~~~~~~~~

Resources and Further Reading

On healing from sexual abuse and trauma

Intimate Deception: Healing the Wounds of Sexual Betrayal, by Dr. Sheri Keffer (Revell, 2018)

On the Threshold of Hope: Opening the Door to Healing for Survivors of Sexual Abuse, by Dr. Diane Langberg (Tyndale House Publishers, 1999).

Suffering and the Heart of God: How Trauma Destroys and Christ Restores, by Dr. Diane Langberg (New Growth Press, 2015).

The Body Keeps the Score: Brain, Mind, and Body in the Healing of Trauma, by Dr. Bessel van der Kolk (Penguin Books, 2014).

The Wall Around Your Heart: How Jesus Heals You When Others Hurt You, by Mary DeMuth (Nelson Books, 2013).

Not Marked: Finding Hope and Healing After Sexual Abuse, by Mary DeMuth (Uncaged Publishing, 2013).

On addressing and overcoming sexual addiction

The Heart of Man, documentary/film directed by Eric Esau, produced by Jason Pamer and Jens Jacob, and executive produced by Chad Veach, Brian Bird, Noel Bouche (Sypher Studios, 2017).

The Heart of Man Participant's Guide, by WM Paul Young, Jackie Hill Perry, Dr. Dan Allender, Jay Stringer, John and Stasi Eldredge (Publisher: Heart of Man, 2017).

Pure Desire: How One Man's Triumph Can Help Others Break Free from Sexual Temptation, by Dr. Ted Roberts (Bethany House Publishing, 2008).

Conquer Series: The Battle Plan for Purity (by KingdomWorks Studios, 2014; Dr. Ted Roberts, Host; Alan Ward, Producer).

Pure Desire Ministries   https://puredesire.org
New Life Ministries   https://newlife.com

On shame and worthiness

Men, Women and Worthiness: The Experience of Shame and the Power of Being Enough, by Dr. Brené Brown (Audible audiobook, 2012).

The Gifts of Imperfection, by Dr. Brené Brown (Hazelden Publishing, 2010).

Rising Strong: How the Ability to Reset Transforms the Way We Live, Love, Parent, and Lead, by Dr. Brené Brown (Penguin Random House, 2015).

Daring Greatly: How the Courage to be Vulnerable Transforms the Way We Live, Love, Parent, and Lead, by Dr. Brené Brown (Avery Publishing, 2015).

Braving the Wilderness: The Quest for True Belonging and the Courage to Stand Alone, by Dr. Brené Brown (Random House Publishing, 2015).

Domestic violence and suicide hotlines

The National Domestic Violence Hotline:
     1-800-799-SAFE   www.thehotline.org

Rape, Abuse, and Incest National Network (RAINN):
    1-800-656-HOPE   https://www.rainn.org

Domestic violence national hotlines and resources:
http://www.feminist.org/911/crisis.html

Domestic violence state hotlines and resources:
http://www.feminist.org/911/crisis_state.html

National Suicide Prevention Lifeline:
    1-800-273-8255
    www.suicidepreventionlifeline.org

Books for the new Christian

Mere Christianity, by C. S. Lewis
Hinds Feet on High Places, by Hannah Hurnard
Lifetime Guarantee: Making Your Christian Life Work and What to Do When it Doesn't, by Bill Gillham (Harvest House Publishers, 1993)

Scripture Verses

Jeremiah 29:11 "For I know the plans I have for you," declares the Lord, "plans to prosper you and not to harm you, plans to give you hope and a future." (NIV)

Hebrews 13:5 . . . God has said, "Never will I leave you; never will I forsake you." (NIV)

Psalm 9:10 Those who know Your name will put their trust in You, for You, O Lord, have not forsaken those who seek You.

Lamentations 3:19-25 I remember my affliction and my wandering . . . my soul is downcast within me. Yet this I call to mind and therefore I have hope: Because of the Lord's great love we are not consumed, for his compassions never fail. They are new every morning; great is your faithfulness. I say to myself, "The Lord is my portion; therefore, I will wait for him." The Lord is good to those whose hope is in him, to the one who seeks him . . . . (NIV)

Isaiah 46:4 Even to your old age and gray hairs I am he, I am he who will sustain you. I have made you and I will carry you; I will sustain you and I will rescue you. (NIV)

Psalm 61:1-3 Hear my cry, O God; listen to my prayer. From the ends of the earth I call to you, I call as my heart grows faint; lead me to the rock that is higher than I. For you have been my refuge, a strong tower . . . . (NIV)

Isaiah 59:1 Surely the arm of the Lord is not too short to save, nor his ear too dull to hear. (NIV)

Psalm 46:1 God is our refuge and strength, an ever-present help in trouble. (NIV)

Psalm 46:10 Be still and know that I am God. (NIV)

Isaiah 30:15 This is what the Sovereign Lord . . . says: "In repentance and rest is your salvation, in quietness and trust is your strength . . ." (NIV)

Exodus 33:14 The Lord replied, "My Presence will go with you, and I will give you rest." (NIV)

Matthew 11:28-29 Come to Me, all who are weary and burdened, and I will give you rest. Take my yoke upon you and learn from me, for I am gentle and humble in heart, and you will find rest for your souls. (NIV)

Psalm 119:105 Your word is a lamp to my feet and a light to my path.

Psalm 23:1-4 The Lord is my shepherd, I shall not want. He makes me lie down in green pastures; He leads me beside quiet waters. He restores my soul. He guides me in the paths of righteousness for His name's sake. Even though I walk through the valley of the shadow of death, I fear no evil, for You are with me; Your rod and Your staff, they comfort me.

Revelations 21:4 He will wipe every tear from their eyes. There will be no more death or mourning or crying or pain, for the old order of things has passed away. (NIV)

Psalms 139:1-4 O Lord, You have searched me and known me. You know when I sit down and when I rise up; You understand my thought from afar. You scrutinize my path and my lying down, and are intimately acquainted with all my ways. Even before there is a word on my tongue, behold, O Lord, You know it all.

Isaiah 40:29-31 Do you not know? Have you not heard? The Lord is the everlasting God, the Creator of the ends of the earth. He will not grow tired or weary, and his understanding no one can fathom. He gives strength to the weary and increases the power of the weak. Even youths grow tired and weary, and young men stumble and fall; but those who hope in the Lord will renew their strength. They will soar on wings like eagles; they will run and not grow weary, they will walk and not be faint. (NIV)

Isaiah 43:1-4 But now, thus says the Lord, who created you . . . and formed you . . . "Fear not, for I have redeemed you; I have called you by your name; you are Mine. When you pass through the waters, I will be with you; and through the rivers, they shall not overflow you. When you walk through the fire, you shall not be burned, nor shall the flame scorch you. For I am the Lord your God . . . your Savior . . . Since you were precious in My sight, . . . and I have loved you . . . ." (NKJV)

Jeremiah 31:33-34 "This is the covenant which I will make with (them). . . ," declares the Lord, "I will put my law in their minds and write it on their hearts. I will be their God, and they will be my people . . . . for I will forgive their iniquity and remember their sin no more." (NIV)

Colossians 1:15-17 The Son is the image of the invisible God, the firstborn over all creation. For in him all things were created: things in heaven and on earth, visible and invisible, whether thrones or powers or rulers or authorities; all things have been created through him and for him. He is before all things, and in him all things hold together. (NIV)

John 1:1-4 In the beginning was the Word, and the Word was with God, and the Word was God. He was in the beginning with God. All things came into being through Him, and apart from Him nothing came into being that has come into being. In Him was life, and the life was the Light of men.

1 John 1:1-3 That which was from the beginning, which we have heard, which we have seen with our eyes, which we have looked at and our hands have touched—this we proclaim concerning the Word of life. The life appeared; we have seen it and testify to it, and we proclaim to you the eternal life, which was with the Father and has appeared to us. We proclaim to you what we have seen and heard, so that you also may have fellowship with us. And our fellowship is with the Father and with his Son, Jesus Christ. (NIV)

Isaiah 12:2 God is my salvation

Isaiah 9:6 For unto us a Child is born, unto us a Son is given; and the government will be upon his shoulder. And his name will be called Wonderful, Counselor, Mighty God, Everlasting Father, Prince of Peace. (NKJV)

Isaiah 53:4-6 Surely our griefs He Himself bore; and our sorrows He carried . . . . He was pierced through for our transgressions, He was crushed for our iniquities; the chastening for our well-being fell upon Him, and by His scourging we are healed. All of us like sheep have gone astray, each of us has turned to his own way; but the Lord has caused the iniquity of us all to fall on Him.

Matthew 1:21 She will bear a Son; and you shall call His name Jesus, for He will save His people from their sins.

John 3:16 For God so loved the world that he gave his one and only Son, that whoever believes in him shall not perish but have eternal life. (NIV)

John 1:29 Behold, the Lamb of God who takes away the sin of the world!

John 10:10b I came that they may have life, and have it abundantly.

John 11:25-26 Jesus said to her, "I am the resurrection and the life. The one who believes in me will live; he who believes in Me will live even if he dies, and everyone who lives and believes in Me will never die. Do you believe this?"

Acts 4:12 And there is salvation in no one else; for there is no other name under heaven that has been given among men by which we must be saved.

Hebrews 11:6 And without faith it is impossible to please Him, for he who comes to God must believe that He is and that He is a rewarder of those who seek Him.

1 John 4:9-10 By this the love of God was manifested in us, that God has sent His only begotten Son into the world so that we might live through Him. In this is love, not that we loved God, but that He loved us and sent His Son to be the propitiation for our sins.

Romans 5:12 Therefore, just as through one man sin entered into the world, and death through sin, and so death spread to all men, because all sinned—

2 Corinthians 5:21 He made Him who knew no sin to be sin on our behalf, so that we might become the righteousness of God in Him.

1 John 1:9 If we confess our sins, He is faithful and righteous to forgive us our sins and to cleanse us from all unrighteousness.

Isaiah 30:18 Therefore the Lord longs to be gracious to you . . . He waits on high to have compassion on you. For the Lord is a God of justice; how blessed are all those who long for Him.

Colossians 2:13-14 When you were dead in your sins and in the uncircumcision of your flesh, God made you alive with Christ. He forgave us all our sins, having canceled the charge of our legal indebtedness, which stood against us and condemned us; he has taken it away, nailing it to the cross. (NIV)

Psalm 32:1, 4-5 Blessed is he whose transgression is forgiven, whose sin is covered . . . day and night Your hand was heavy upon me . . . . I acknowledged my sin to You, and my iniquity I did not hide; I said, "I will confess my transgressions to the Lord"; and You forgave the guilt of my sin.

Psalms 103:12 As far as the east is from the west, so far has He removed our transgressions from us.

Romans 8:1 Therefore there is now no condemnation for those who are in Christ Jesus.

Ephesians 1:7-8 In Him we have redemption through His blood, the forgiveness of our trespasses, according to the riches of His grace which He lavished on us.

Ephesians 2:4-5, 8-9 But God, being rich in mercy, because of His great love with which He loved us, even when we were dead in our transgressions, made us alive together with Christ . . . . For by grace you have been saved through faith; and that not of yourselves, it is the gift of God; not as a result of works, so that no one may boast.

1 Peter 1:3 Blessed be the God and Father of our Lord Jesus Christ, who according to His great mercy has caused us to be born again to a living hope through the resurrection of Jesus Christ from the dead . . . .

2 Corinthians 5:17 Therefore if anyone is in Christ, he is a new creature; the old things passed away; behold, new things have come.

Galatians 2:20 I have been crucified with Christ; and it is no longer I who live, but Christ lives in me; and the life which I now live in the flesh I live by faith in the Son of God, who loved me and gave Himself up for me.

Romans 6:6-7 . . . . knowing this, that our old self was crucified with Him, in order that our body of sin might be done away with, so that we would no longer be slaves to sin; for he who has died is freed from sin.

Galatians 4:7 Therefore you are no longer a slave, but a son; and if a son, then an heir through God.

Titus 2:1 For the grace of God has appeared, bringing salvation to all men . . . .

Psalms 13:5 I have trusted in Your lovingkindness; my heart shall rejoice in Your salvation.

Luke 10:20b Rejoice that your names are recorded in heaven.

Ephesians 1:3-6 Praise be to the God and Father of our Lord Jesus Christ, who has blessed us in the heavenly realms with every spiritual blessing in Christ. For he chose us in him before the creation of the world to be holy and blameless in his sight. In love he predestined us for adoption as sons through Jesus Christ, in accordance with his pleasure and will — to the praise of his glorious grace, which he has freely given us in the One he loves. (NIV)

Romans 12:2 And do not be conformed to this world, but be transformed by the renewing of your mind, so that you may prove what the will of God is, that which is good and acceptable and perfect.

Colossians 3:1-3 Therefore since you have been raised up with Christ, keep seeking the things above, where Christ is, seated at the right hand of God. Set your mind on the things above, not on the things that are on earth. For you have died and your life is hidden with Christ in God. (NIV)

John 15:5 I am the vine, you are the branches; he who abides in Me and I in him, he bears much fruit, for apart from Me you can do nothing.

2 Corinthians 12:9 But he said to me, "My grace is sufficient for you, for my power is made perfect in weakness." (NIV)

John 14:20 In that day you will know that I am in My Father, and you in Me, and I in you.

Philippians 4:13 I can do all things through Christ who strengthens me. (NKJV)

Philippians 4:6-7 Be anxious for nothing, but in everything by prayer and supplication with thanksgiving let your requests be made known to God. And the peace of God, which surpasses all comprehension, will guard your hearts and your minds in Christ Jesus.

Hebrews 4:15-16 For we do not have a high priest who cannot sympathize with our weaknesses, but One who has been tempted in all things as we are, yet without sin. Therefore let us draw near with confidence to the throne of grace, so that we may receive mercy and find grace to help in time of need.

Romans 8:35, 38-39 Who will separate us from the love of Christ? Will tribulation, or distress, or persecution, or famine, or nakedness, or peril, or sword? . . . But in all these things we overwhelmingly conquer through Him who loved us. For I am convinced that neither death, nor life, nor angels, nor principalities, nor things present, nor things to come, nor powers, nor height, nor depth, nor any other created thing, will be able to separate us from the love of God, which is in Christ Jesus our Lord.

Romans 8:28 And we know that God causes all things to work together for good to those who love God, to those who are called according to His purpose.

John 11:40 Then Jesus said, "Did I not tell you that if you believe, you will see the glory of God?" (NIV)

Romans 15:13 May the God of hope fill you with all joy and peace as you trust in him, so that you may overflow with hope by the power of the Holy Spirit. (NIV)

Numbers 6:24-25 The Lord bless you and keep you; the Lord make his face shine on you and be gracious to you . . . .

Ephesians 3:20-22 Now to him who is able to do immeasurably more than all we ask or imagine, according to his power that is at work within us, to him be glory in the church and in Christ Jesus throughout all generations, for ever and ever! Amen. (NIV)

About the Author

Shawn Ward is a graduate of U.C., Berkeley, Haas School of Business and has worked in the fields of accounting, finance, and real estate. More importantly, she has loved being a mother and taught as a home-school educator for thirteen years, seeing all three of her daughters through university and some graduate school. She is passionate about sharing her love of family and her real-life journey as told in *HIS Story*. Shawn's prayer is to bring enlightenment and hope—in a thoughtfully courageous and sensitively transparent manner—to others, women and men alike, who find themselves in marriages suffering from loss, addiction, and devastation. She lives in the beautiful Carson Valley in northern Nevada and the Front Range in northern Colorado.

Made in the USA
San Bernardino, CA
14 February 2020

64506852R00129